To the memory of William Le Messurier

Tall Building: Imagining the Skyscraper

Scott Johnson

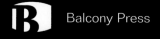 Balcony Press

The Building of the Tower of Babel, Kunsthistorisches
Museum, Vienna, 1563. Pieter Brueghel the Elder.

Project for a Monument to the Third International, 1919.
Vladimir Tatlin.

The universe (which others call the Library) is composed of an indefinite and perhaps infinite number of hexagonal galleries, with vast air shafts between, surrounded by very low railings. From any of the hexagons one can see, interminably, the upper and lower floors. The distribution of the galleries is invariable ... Also through here passes a spiral stairway, which sinks abysmally and soars upwards to remote distances.

— Jorge Luis Borges, *The Library of Babel*

One day, and probably soon, we need some recognition of what above all is lacking in our big cities: quiet and wide, expansive places for reflection. Places with long, elevated cloisters for bad or all too sunny weather where no shouting or noises of carriages can reach and where good manners would prohibit even priests from praying aloud-buildings and sites that would altogether give expression to the sublimity of thoughtfulness and of stepping aside.

— Friedrich Nietzsche, *The Gay Science*

What interests me is architecture as monster, those objects that have been catapulted into the city, from someplace else.

— Jean Baudrillard, *The Singular Objects of Architecture*

Contents

9 Preface

11 Prologue

17 Chapter 1 — Inevitable Skyscraper

Profit and Imagination
Context and Consensus
The Archetype
Commerce and Its Effects

57 Chapter 2 — The Enrichment of Vertical Space

Trajectories
Radical Invention
Ground Zero

107 Chapter 3 — The Environmental Skyscraper

The Energy Dilemma
Norman Foster
Ken Yeang

143 Chapter 4 — Designer Skyscraper

Madison Avenue
High Hospitality
Variations

175 Chapter 5 — FutureTall

Asia
The Middle East
Russia

211 Chapter 6 — Art Skyscrapers

Minimalism Three Times
Domesticities and the Informational Tower

263 Bibliography
269 Photography Credits
273 Index
281 Acknowledgements
283 The Author

Preface

Scott Johnson's book comes at a period when there is great public excitement about tall buildings. On the one hand, there is that overworked — and often misused — word ICON that is applied to them. And on the other, there is the continued wish to coerce groups and organizations into a state of proximity.

Somehow, the notion of the 'ground-scraper' has never really taken off. Even those lovely Scandinavian company headquarters that drift gently down to the fjord just feel like continuations of the suburbs that they adjoin.

No, the skyscraper is still the stuff of Heroes. Superman and Superwoman can aspire to the executive floor, or even higher. The timid out-of-towner can suitably palpitate on entering the auspicious lobby. The only problem is, as a designer, how to make your tall box different from the rest? More likely than not, the proposition is based around those overwhelmingly logical rules of access and daylight. Not only with predictable distances of the surrounding body of the building, but with predictable (and again, logical) heights of room. The fashion designer must face the same dilemmas: the body is but a body with all its failings, so how to dress it?

Between forty and twenty years ago, we seemed to be in a rut; eschewing the mannerisms of the old 'Woolworth Building' skyscrapers, we created endless, if circumspect, slabs. Arguments about decoration tended to be rather marginal; at least until Philip Johnson went so far as to put a giant pediment on the top of one.

Thus, the importance of this book is that the beginnings of a serious typological and conceptual change are to be found. Disarmingly and without rhetoric, Johnson leads us by the hand towards the most marvelous and inventive piles that are now beginning to emerge with the onset of the twenty-first century. The Phare Tower of Morphosis, or some of Ken Yeang's inventions look at the high building as an organism, as a collective element for a new life. They anticipate a time when the logic of the standard floor will be a rejected tyranny of mean thinking. Perhaps this is my dream that I am overlaying upon the gradual, collective evidence and surreptitious implication of a book that in other hands would just be a dictionary of the commercially successful block.

Heights — and the dream of the vertical city — inspire many of the projects within. And from Tatlin's open tower to Foster's winding Saint Mary Axe, there is surely the search for the three-dimensional city as well.

It is intriguing that with the attacks on the World Trade Center, the first knee-jerk reaction (certainly from the direction of the naturally timid), was to question the role, purpose and morality of the tall building. This reaction lasted only a few weeks and yet it seems to have had a galvanizing effect. The new skyscrapers step forward with a new stride, unafraid to be even taller, or even more encompassing.

What a fascinating read.

— Sir Peter Cook

Prologue

As the three quotations at the front of this book suggest, distinct temperaments frequently address the same topic, in this case, the tall building. Whatever it may be as a physical fact, the tall building looms larger as a figment of the imagination, as a primary vehicle for projecting one's vision of expedience, transcendence, ambition or dominance. The image of the skyscraper has been made and remade infinite times through the prevalence of news programs, literature, film, and all forms of our now global media. The images of distant skyscrapers from far corners of the earth are brought to us in an endless stream, asserting themselves, yet morphing and recalling the blur of other skyscrapers we seem to remember having seen somewhere else before. Paradoxically, as the building type continues to develop greater levels of complexity, encompassing subtler technologies, and designed to address specific and fundamentally different cultures, the image, that is to say, the idea, of the skyscraper in the public mind seems to become simpler, more omnipresent, and more consumable.

Terminology is curious. While a tall building is any habitable structure which is in its essence vertical, the word skyscraper is both physical and evocative. In English it brings to mind the language of modern rhetorical poetry in posing the query, "how high must we be to scrape the sky?" A wide range of other terms describes this building type, and each carries its own inferences or makes its own edits: tower, vertical building, high-rise. Perhaps the most sensory and divine is predictably the Italian *grattacielo*, which is imbued with the Italian onomatopoeia for scratching and the semantic ambiguity of sky and heaven.

Two years ago, I completed a book entitled *The Big Idea: Criticality and Practice in Contemporary Architecture.* The aim of that project was to mediate in some way the application of recent theoretical studies in architecture and the actual practice of architecture. The book was in fact a guidebook for a way to think about and build a critically considered practice. Its text navigated the constructs of various theoretical positions and identified ways in which these positions actually inform the design and construction of major works of architecture. The contrary position, which holds that contemporary theory and practice fail to inform each other, or are even oppositional, while in vogue, appears widely unfounded when one investigates the architectural output of critical and progressive practices. For me, this realization grew out of my own parallel experience of academic teaching and studies on the one hand, and the practice of designing buildings — many of them tall buildings — on the other.

In writing that book and examining the territory of architectural theory from the post-World War II period to the present, one of the grand contours in that terrain appeared to be the broad shift in thinking from what has been generally described as structuralism (a conceptual strategy that emerged in the mid-twentieth century and paralleled the development of modernism) to post-structuralism (a subsequent development and reaction to what had preceded it, and often subsumed under the more general heading of a cultural postmodernism). That led, as I outlined in *The Big Idea,* to the notion of the end of theory, or post-criticality as it has been called. In its most succinct form, post-criticality suggests that historiography as a verifiable narrative or documentary is at best a polemic, the outcome of an equivocating struggle for power by the tellers of history that cannot purport to be either accurate or relevant to a critical point of view. With the advent of post-structuralism and the recognition in the Western mainstream of an expanding range of alternative and counter cultures, came a reworking of structuralism's initial premise. Recalling the original implications of Noam Chomsky's work in linguistics, and Ferdinand de Saussure's before him, something fundamental and eternal in the essence of human language was proposed to exist and this "deep structure" provided bedrock for infinite permutations of expression. The post-structuralist coalitions that assembled soon thereafter inverted that formulation, stating that deep structure was a myth, that those infinite permutations were not rooted in any singular and intrinsic human character.

In the realm of architecture, this newfound relativity initiated a diaspora of more specialized positions with names such as metabolism, historicism, neo-classicism, regionalism, populism, deconstructivism and back again to another, and this time revisionary, modernism. Newly reinforced with digital imaging tools, global practices, and the establishment of a media and marketing elite, this newer and revised modern architecture, originally conceived to be some kind of socially beneficial force for the masses, was now seen by many to be torn from its original socialist moorings and flung into the capitalist arena. Modernism on the rebound, they said, had been recontextualized in a world of global markets, capital flows and media omnipresence. Notwithstanding these tectonic shifts acting upon the practice of architecture, certain critical practitioners have succeeded in producing work that poses difficult questions and compels us to live in the present. It now seems natural to acknowledge that claims of the end of history, the severance of theory and practice, and the failure of architecture as an intentional and potentially moral operation, were premature.

After reviewing all this, and concluding with modest suggestions for restorative links between thinking and doing, I completed *The Big Idea* and prepared myself for a rest and a change of scenery. I would design some new buildings, teach classes, deliver a number of lectures and prepare an altogether new project, one in which I have had a longstanding interest, a book on the most current matters surrounding the design of tall buildings. For nearly two years, I collected and reviewed all the literature available on them. Among the many recent book projects I studied were oversized picture books exhibiting the mostly outward and visual qualities of tall buildings. A number of museums and recognized contributors in the field had produced exhibitions with catalogues on specific case studies of tall buildings they considered to be of note. There were also many books which had chosen to focus on the technical strategies that have allowed architects and engineers to stabilize skyscrapers as they pursue greater heights. Finally, I found a steady stream of periodical literature addressing the topic, reminding me that skyscrapers are popular phenomena with staying power.

Today it seems clear to observers of the material world that few manmade objects escape the aura of cultural signification. In a world of dense commercial marketing, a woman's handbag can be, now more than ever, a communicator of discernment, lifestyle and affluence. In a world of product proliferation and in consideration of the totality of acquired meanings, the handbag's existence owes less to its performance as a carrier of goods, and significantly more to what it purports to say about its owner. Commercial success and the drive for self-expression have become codependent in the extreme. In both the post-industrial and developing nations of the world, this could easily be said of water, wine, apparel, automobile, residence, travel destination, indeed all those things which are consumable. Now that communications, material production and personal travel are truly global phenomena, so have these acts of signification acquired a global audience. It is safe to say now, and it is a consistent theme in these writings, that the modern skyscraper has clearly entered this postmodern realm of broad cultural signification.

Guy Nordenson, a gifted and articulate structural engineer of skyscrapers, refers to the tall building as metaphor in his introductory essay to the 2004 *Tall Buildings* exhibition catalogue for New York's Museum of Modern Art. Nordenson employs the term metaphor in a different context than that to which I refer, assigning collective, industrial and historic meaning to the skyscraper as he briefly outlines the chronological development of the building type. In pursuit of a sense of collective history, he concludes his thoughts on the skyscraper by referring to the so-called "standard model," a theory first formulated in the 1970s within the field of subatomic particle physics. The model originally codified specific relationships between matter particles. It created a high degree of reliability in predicting the outcome of experimentation, yet left vast tracts of science open to intuitive reasoning. Nordenson takes on this standard model metaphor to describe democracy in action, the industrial methods of the automobile industry, and, ultimately, the historic design of tall buildings. Nordenson's metaphor places the current intersection of established engineering science and innovation in skyscraper design within a collective and historic context.

My idea of the skyscraper as metaphor is different. Here, metaphor points to the role that the tall building has come to play within today's highly semiotic world. This world is largely defined by the codependence of industrial production and the consumption of cultural artifacts. The ability for a physical object to be imbued with associative meaning implies wide-ranging qualities to its inhabitants or owners and both conflates and differentiates human groupings.

Perhaps the notion has always been with me that there is no artifact more synthetic and comprehensive in our contemporary world than the skyscraper as a symbol of cultural production. The myriad choices of material selection, formal language, structural technique and the technological "borrowing" inherent in the building type are informative in the context of the skyscraper as cultural icon, telling us not just how we build, but why and for whom we build. In this telling, both the ideas underlying a particular skyscraper, as well as the design and production of it, come together in our imagining of the tall building. And so the critical dialectic I thought I had set aside in my prior book, raised its head again. And the lens through which I believe we must view the recent development of the tall building as an artifact of physical culture, restates the abiding problems of structuralism, post-structuralism and the prospect of post-theory.

Strangely, while references in books have been made, and news and magazine articles abound, the first book that I know to take on this aspect of the subject, is the quite recent *Iconic Building*, a 2005 publication by Charles Jencks. The book's cover displays Norman Foster's Swiss Re building irreverently blasting off as if commencing some astral launch and many of the "iconic" buildings inside the book are tall buildings. Jencks' sporadic reportage is perhaps indicative of the fact that the cultural mapping of iconography in buildings is a relatively new topic and we are only now beginning to navigate it.

Tall Building: Imagining the Skyscraper, then, is a series of topical essays reflecting the peculiar themes that characterize the tall building at this moment. We begin with a discussion of the recurring and inevitable forces that brought about the skyscraper, from the persistently commercial realities of a burgeoning American marketplace to the wide-ranging and theoretical proposals of European architects who had built little. A reflection follows on the unique challenges and promises associated with vertically organized mixed-use space. Then, we explore two distinctly different architectural practices that have made environmental sensitivity their hallmarks. This is followed by commentary on the cult of design, designer and lifestyle and its effects on the skyscraper habitat. Then, a review of developing cities, many in Asia and the Middle East, and the place of super-tall buildings within them. Finally, we conclude with a look at the image of the tall building as appropriated by various artists, visionaries and critical thinkers beyond the physical constraints generally associated with architecture. Though the topicality and brevity of this book deny any attempt at defining a comprehensive history, I confess to having made a series of choices to include certain buildings, architects, and works of art which I feel approximate a substantive and ongoing legacy in the design of the skyscraper.

It has been suggested that nearly half of the world's skyscrapers have been built since the year 2000. It appears certain that, for many reasons, the current pace will continue into the foreseeable future. With so many skyscrapers presently in design and construction, it is difficult to imagine a critique that is anything but instantly obsolete. Nevertheless, with history's authority in doubt and the relation of theory to creative production under review, an examination of the tall building as cultural artifact may give us a telling glimpse into the universe of our own intentions.

— Scott Johnson

Chapter 1

Inevitable Skyscraper

The Dialectics of Profit and Imagination

The genesis and early history of the skyscraper is grounded in the American cultures
of urban real estate, commercialism and industrialization. The city of Chicago's preeminent
role has long been established. Fig. 1.1 Its central
location at the confluence of Midwestern agriculture and industry, and the early construction
of transportation lines that moved those goods
in all directions ensured that role. In the latter
half of the nineteenth century, a number of
important events converged in Chicago to
promote the development of the tall building.
Rising and speculative land values within the
city center, the development of high-strength
steel, the beginnings of an effective curtain
wall technology, and the invention of the elevator all came together to confirm Chicago as the
home of America's first skyscrapers. With the
devastating fire of 1871, an urgent and unique
opportunity arose to rebuild most of the city
at precisely the moment when these new
developments could advance the building type.
   The proliferation of early skyscrapers in
New York City occurred almost immediately
thereafter, subject to its own pressures to
provide commercial space. As the principal
domestic port of immigration and the center
for most international trade, New York's need
for commercial office space was enormous
and ultimately greater than that of Chicago.

Most of this construction, in the nineteenth and early twentieth centuries, was located in Lower Manhattan at a time when more than ninety percent of all skyscrapers in both cities were speculative commercial office buildings. Original block sizes available to real estate developers in each city were characteristically different. The standard size in Chicago measured 360 by 320 feet, bisected by a longitudinal alley. Fig. 1.2 The tip of Manhattan, with its small colonial parcels, its irregular street patterns, and the high cost of assembling multiple contiguous lots, led to smaller floor plates with higher land costs.[1] Fig. 1.4

Chicago's financial panic of 1893, which involved an oversupply of office space and wide failures within the lending community, led to an immediate 130-foot height limit on all buildings throughout the city. New York City, on the other hand, where there was no height limit and iron-frame construction had been allowed by its municipal building code since 1889, had numerous buildings in the 600 to 700 foot height range. Fig. 1.3 Though architects in both cities worked with comparable technologies and materials, these different conditions led to fundamentally different building typologies, broader and lower buildings in Chicago with narrower and taller buildings in New York. As proximity to natural light and air remained important for functional office space, distances between the perimeter wall and the interior circulation core in these buildings generally hovered between twenty-four and twenty-eight feet. As parcel sizes were generally larger in Chicago and other cities, and only occasionally so in New York, light wells were designed into the wider buildings to maximize light and air to the interior, while the exterior wall was located at the property line, maximizing use of the site's dimension in pursuit of the highest possible density.

Chicago architect Louis Sullivan's oft quoted line from his 1896 essay, "The Tall Office Building Artistically Considered," while defining his own personal strategies for addressing the design of tall Midwestern buildings, could well have been applicable to the characteristically taller buildings of New York. "It must be every inch a proud and soaring thing, rising in sheer exultation that from bottom to top it is a unit without a single dissenting line."[2] Practically speaking, for Sullivan and many other designers in Chicago and New York, this mantra could be translated into the identifiably tripartite organization of the building's exterior into base, shaft and capital. Fig. 1.5 Not unlike the design of a classical column, each new skyscraper seemed grounded in a highly articulated lower floor incorporating at least one monumental entry, above which a

vertical organization of windows and solid walls appeared, the top of which was crowned by a cornice or entablature which outlined its highly identifiable silhouette on the horizon.

We now know that it was a particularly negative and unanimous response to a series of tall buildings, which were both massive and extremely dense, that caused New York's 1916 zoning ordinance to be written, the city's first legislation to control the height and bulk of tall buildings. Unlike the city's "spire" skyscrapers, the Singer, Metropolitan Life and Woolworth buildings, each slender and successive holder of the record for the world's tallest tower, a new series of alarmingly dense buildings was being conceived. The largest of these, and what came to be the most pivotal, was the Equitable Life Assurance Society Building. Fig. 1.6 Completed in 1915, at 542 feet tall, it was the fifth tallest tower in New York, and, with 1.2 million square feet of leasable space, it was the largest office building in the world. Buildings such as these, in their extreme scale, blocked views, sunlight and air from other buildings as well as from the public right-of-way. Ultimately and importantly, the community of planners and landlords perceived that they decreased the value of nearby commercial property. In response, the City of New York promptly wrote high-rise building guidelines into its zoning ordinance, enforcing various setbacks and height limitations based upon lot size and street widths, producing buildings with broad podiums and stepping back in the lower midsections to narrow stepped shafts above. Fig. 1.7

These guidelines, intended to mediate a skyscraper's impact on the public's experience of the city, stayed in place for more than forty years and most other major American cities enacted similar legislation. In the hands of skilled designers, these wedding cake skyscrapers evoked a kind of archetypal, even decorative style. No images expressed the romantic potential of these buildings so much as paintings and drawings by Hugh Ferriss, a trained architect who became best known for his artwork describing the new design guidelines and many of the buildings of his time. Fig. 1.8 Even the winning entry to the much celebrated Chicago Tribune Tower competition, an ecclesiastically ornamental skyscraper noted for the fineness of its detailing, and its distinctive bottom, middle and top, appeared reminiscent of both Sullivan's dictum as well as the popularity of New York City's spires and setbacks. Fig. 1.9 Additionally, the architects for this most important Chicago building were New York's John Mead Howells and Raymond Hood. Many of New York City's most iconic buildings built over the next twenty years would be designed by Hood within the lingering constraints of the 1916 zoning ordinance. Mythic skyscrapers including Shreve, Lamb & Harmon's Empire State Building, William van Alen's Chrysler Building, and Hood's Rockefeller Center were all designed within these guidelines, transforming the familiar profile into an early modern archetype.

Even as the trend for American skyscrapers spread beyond New York and Chicago after 1916, these urban towers were generally conceived as infill buildings within a larger, less dense, urban fabric. Height and bulk regulations held that the public realm was primary. Only after a skyscraper was set back, reduced to an acceptable breadth, and began to ascend to its crown did it have license to fully express its unique identity. New York became the first city to mediate between a publicly defined vision of the city and the capitalist drive to convert high-rise real estate into maximum income. The lower floor of each skyscraper acted as the street-wall of the public right-of-way, the ground-level entrance and lobby were the ceremonial extension of the sidewalk, and a building facing a public park became the metaphoric tower on the town square, all the while maximizing density and securing its worth in the commercial marketplace.

While the image of the urban American skyscraper was both consolidating and spreading, a different strain of largely theoretical urbanism was forming in Europe, a force not grown from overpowering capitalist exigencies but from a set of intersecting philosophical, social and aesthetic discourses. These critiques which began as books, manifestos, exhibitions, and occasional proposals, would later influence and ultimately overtake the standard view of the American skyscraper, rewriting its role in the fabric of the city.

It could be said that no one put forward a vision of the early modern skyscraper more forcefully and persistently within a radical vision for redesigning the city than Le Corbusier (né Charles-Edouard Jeanneret), the Swiss/French architect and artist. For the author of "a machine for living in," the skyscraper was a singular icon that celebrated the object quality of the new industrial world. As a physical program, Le Corbusier's conception of the tall building was the antithesis of the Manhattan skyscraper. Whereas in New York the densities and cumulative qualities of the extant city, the infill nature of towers, and the fact that the success of the pedestrian ground plane relied on a full range of programmatic events in the base of tall buildings, the logic of Le Corbusier's towers reversed this paradigm, conceptualizing the skyscraper as a single, programmatically complete object, sitable in a theoretical urban landscape of gardens and arterials. Fig. 1.10 – Fig. 1.12 Unlike New York's codependence between tower and city, Le Corbusier's tower became the city as object, and was freed to redraw its relations with other urban systems, namely nature and transportation. Geometry and repetition became the two formal devices he employed to create his master plan. In his work, he borrowed from the new logic of a functionally ordered industrial society, seeded it with the scale of a Haussmannian Paris, and created an intellectual vision in which he felt buildings, as objects, could meet nature, as vast gardens. These notions of the tall building persisted in various forms throughout Le Corbusier's work in South America and Algiers, and arrived in fullness with his Unité d'Habitation in Marseilles toward the end of his life.

Curiously, Le Corbusier's unpublished first book written about 1910, entitled *The Building of Cities,* was concerned with the "aesthetic of the street," and was much influenced by Camillo Sitte's ground-breaking 1889 book, *City Design According to Its Artistic Principles.* Moving to Paris soon thereafter, his vision for the skyscraper and its relation to the city evolved over four decades, beginning in earnest in 1921 when he was commissioned by Marcel Temporal to prepare an exhibition for Paris' 1922 Autumn Salon. A Contemporary City for Three Million Inhabitants constituted his first fully delineated vision of the organization of the modern city and the place of the tall building in it. Fig. 1.11 The project clearly drew insights from Tower City, the modern Parisian architect Auguste Perret's earlier formulation for the city as a field of skyscrapers.

The decade following World War I was an enormously fertile time for Le Corbusier with little actual building but dense theoretical work, books and sweeping proposals. Generally elaborated during the 1920s as his Green City, the Plan Voisin of 1925 adapted his principles, begun with the City for Three Million, to a plan for Paris. Fig. 1.10 The year 1923, had seen his radical architectural manifesto, *Vers une Architecture,* into print, followed up in 1925 by *Urbanisme,* which explored the role of architecture in the city.

By this time, Le Corbusier's design theory of The Five Points, an outline of the architectural elements he introduced in 1926, and which remained for him the new paradigm for most of his career, was fully identified. Functionally articulated and machinelike in their clarity, they included the structural grid, the repetition of floors, the organization of vertical circulation, a lightweight curtain wall and functional use of the roof. All these features were represented to be the basis for the buildings in the Plan Voisin, which included cruciform glass skyscrapers 220 meters high, spaced 400 meters apart. This was the approximate distance between Paris Metro stations, sited in a super grid of highways and vast gardens. Unlike the cumulative architectural history that was Manhattan, Le Corbusier's plan for Paris was theoretical, Cartesian, biaxial and unyielding to the character of the historic cityscape. Though his new definition of the skyscraper presumed to incorporate the programmatic vitality of the city, its architectural image as an extruded glass cruciform was hermetic and highly neutral. Fig. 1.12 The towers, spaced at great distance, were undifferentiated from bottom to middle to top, and the pedestrian ground plane took on a picturesque and spacious quality, with none of the social energy apparent in the more compressed historic city.

In 1929, Le Corbusier took an extended trip to South America where he made city planning proposals for Buenos Aires, Rio de Janeiro and Montevideo. His experiences there sensitized him to the potential for both topography and solar orientation as significant generators of architectural form. His sketches from the period display interest in orienting buildings both planimetrically and elevationally with respect to particular natural features (mountains, water, coastlines and the sun). Roadways became fused with buildings rather than being segregated and restricted to a super grid, buildings were bent to create a more intimate relationship with the landscape. Symmetries were eliminated. And the orientation of tall buildings became heliotropic with respect to what he called the "dictating sun." All this growth and design development appears to have had immediate effect on his Radiant City plan of the same year, where land use zoning is more fully integrated and the biaxiality of the Plan Voisin is jettisoned for a linear and organic primary axis. The cruciform skyscraper had been modified to allow sun to illuminate all sides of the building, tendencies which continue to develop in his later work in Algiers and the Unité d'Habitation.

One of the less well-documented visionaries who contributed importantly to the image of the early skyscraper and its place in the city was the Berlin architect and theorist, Ludwig Hilberseimer, a friend and colleague of Ludwig Mies van der Rohe. His understanding of the workings of the modern city and its problems was prescient as he described it in his 1923 essay, "On the Urban Planning Problem of the Metropolis." "So the metropolis appears primarily as a creation of omnipotent big capital, an expression of capital's vast power and anonymity, a city type with unique socioeconomic and mass-psychological features, allowing for both the greatest isolation and the densest crowding of its inhabitants. The hectic pace of a life rhythm accelerated a thousandfold suppresses everything specific and individual. In certain features all metropolises are so similar that it is possible to speak of the internationality of their physiognomy."[3] Hilberseimer goes on to predict that the issue of traffic would become the "alpha and omega of the entire city organism,"[4] a perspective from which he would criticize Le Corbusier's City for Three Million.

With respect to architectural design, Hilberseimer stated: "A city layout based on geometry is in accord with the basic principles of all architecture, of which the straight line and right angle have always been the noblest elements." Looking to cultural traditions and thinking of tall buildings, he said, "Shaping huge masses according to a universal law, suppressing diversity, is what Nietzsche took to be the very definition of style. The universal, the law itself, is honored and brought to the fore; the exception, conversely, is set aside. Nuance is erased. Mass becomes the master, chaos is forced to take on form, logically, unambiguously, mathematics, law."[5] From today's perspective, Hilberseimer's words may elicit an ominously static vision of the city, but his clarity of mind allowed his work to stand out as an important critique of the emerging modern city and the proposals of his various colleagues.

In 1924, Hilberseimer visited Le Corbusier in Paris and reviewed his City for Three Million of two years earlier. Returning to Berlin and referring to his colleague's plan, he stated lucidly, "The solution to the traffic problem cannot be arrived at through an increase in the possibilities of circulation, but only by making traffic as unnecessary as possible. The city is dying today not because it is not geometrical, as Le Corbusier believes, but because it is not organic. Geometric order is undoubtedly a fundamental means to give form to the city, but is always only a means. It is never an end in itself."[6]

In consideration of the interrelated issues of density and traffic, and what he had seen in Paris, Hilberseimer produced three drawings to describe his own Project for a High-Rise City. The significance of the proposal, which was designed to accommodate Berlin's population of 4 million, was its integration of multiple uses in a single building, creating a strategy to "organically" reduce the need for transit. While Le Corbusier's theoretical drawings were planimetrically generated, the insights of Hilberseimer's scheme resided in the building section. Below grade, on four underground levels, the subway and train tracks were proposed to run between stations measuring 600 meters apart, setting the length of each block. At the ground level, wide streets for cars and service traffic were shown accessing massive five-story podium office buildings, on top of which were pedestrian sidewalks and bridges lined by a tall retail floor at the base of fifteen-story slender residential slabs above. The long axes of the towers are oriented to the north and south providing sunlight over the course of the day onto both facades and into the open space between towers.

Another visionary European voice in the early formulation of the tall building was Germany's Ludwig Mies van der Rohe. One year before the exhibition of the competition for the Chicago Tribune Tower, and Le Corbusier's City for Three Million from which the cruciform skyscraper emerged, another competition for a skyscraper on Berlin's Friedrichstrasse was held. Fig. 1.13 – Fig. 1.15 While the 1921 event engaged the talents of established architects, including Hans Poelzig, Hugo Haring and Hans Scharoun, the thirty-five-year-old van der Rohe submitted a surprising, and ultimately influential, scheme for the triangular commercial site. Ignoring the competition specifications, which required a provision for open space and setbacks at the corners of the property, van der Rohe produced a series of charcoal drawings depicting an all-glass extrusion, faceted in plan to respond to the triangular site and broken into three smaller towers nested about a round circulation core. The drawings depicted both the transparency of a monolithic glass wall which expressed the thin floor slabs within, as well as the shadows and reflections which would be cast off the naturally reflective and multifaceted walls. While van der Rohe appeared to have exploited the sculptural and visual complexities of the physical building, programmatically, his proposal was a simple vertical extrusion with twenty identical floors.

Mies van der Rohe shared the Expressionist infatuation with crystals and faceted shapes seen in the work of Bruno Taut, Paul Scheerbart, Hans Poelzig and Hermann Finsterlin. Contrary to the overall planning basis for Le Corbusier's cruciform towers or the model of the conventional American skyscraper, he seemed to be neither interested in the theoretical aspects of city building, nor did he employ decorative facades to recontextualize history. His own motivations at this juncture appear to have been vacillating between the pure aestheticism of the German Expressionist ethos and an obsession with representing the industrial tectonics of the building in a modern and intellectually transparent way. Just as Le Corbusier was experimenting with the city plan, inclusive of tall buildings to symbolize the New Age, van der Rohe was employing the skyscraper as its symbolic and ritual object. In a 1922 publication featuring his

Friedrichstrasse tower, he explained his strategy while attacking conventional tall buildings of the day. "Only skyscrapers under construction reveal the bold constructive thoughts, and then the impression of the high-reaching steel skeletons is overpowering. With the raising of the walls, this impression is completely destroyed; the constructive thought, the necessary basis for artistic form-giving, is annihilated and frequently smothered by a meaningless and trivial jumble of forms."[7]

Several months later, van der Rohe designed a second skyscraper for a pentagonal site at the intersection of two major streets. The thirty-story tower was once again a pure vertical extrusion of glass. However this time, the shape took on an amoeba-like form in plan, minutely faceted as if under the spell of a Hugo Häring or Jean Arp. Fig. 1.16 – Fig. 1.17 Once again, his representations of the tower exhibit the same ambivalence to transparency versus monolithic surface that the earlier skyscraper had shown. His handmade model was built with highly transparent skin, making visible an interior structural cage of impossibly thin floor slabs and infrequent columns, while his charcoal and crayon drawings appear opaque, exhibiting instead the changing reflections on each vertical strand of window-wall. Van der Rohe's aesthetic interests were consistently winning out over any realistic concern for function or technology. He spoke as a modern sculptor when he said, "My experiments with a glass model helped me along the way and I soon recognized that by employing glass, it is not an effect of light and shadow one wants to achieve but a rich interplay of light reflections."[8]

In these early years Mies van der Rohe pursued the design of the skyscraper as a form which operated within the existing city fabric as transformational, iconic, even aberrant. Although he frequently spoke of the beauty of construction made visible, he saw the skyscraper as a physical artifact which he aestheticized in striking, yet nuanced, ways. None of these proposals were built, but they remain firmly written in our collective memory and have been revisited by architects many times since, as high-performance materials and technologies have continued to develop.

While Le Corbusier is said to have been enormously affected by the historic urbanism of New York City, the seed of modernism which he would plant in the city would be a sketch for the design and construction of the United Nations Secretariat, completed in 1950. He had visited New York much earlier and was reported to be impressed with Rockefeller Center, and yet on the whole he was generally and persistently critical of New York skyscrapers, which he considered "misshapen adolescents of the machine age … handled nonsensically as the result of a deplorably romantic city ordinance."[9] He was, of course, referring to the 1916 zoning ordinance still in effect. In fact, high-rise architecture was in a transitional state. Following World War II, the new building boom saw scores of buildings, which, while following the "wedding cake" formulas of the zoning law, had migrated away from the historicist and romantic styles of the pre-war period. Tall buildings along commercial Park Avenue, for example, rose over their full sites to a height of 150 feet and then stepped back repeatedly until there was no viable floor area left to occupy. The elevations of these buildings were generally finished in grey limestone or other similar stone with horizontal ribbon windows. Fig. 1.18 These innocuous pyramids multiplied easily as they lacked any certain ambition and were less expensive to build than their highly decorative predecessors.

With this as the background for current tall building activity in the city, Le Corbusier was commissioned by the U.N. to design its building on an expansive East River site. Fig. 1.19 Political developments, however, placed his conceptual work within the hands of an international committee of architects under the leadership of Wallace K. Harrison. This became the first major building of scale in the city that fully embraced the geometric and sculptural power of the modern movement with its functional articulation of uses, in this case, the Secretariat and the General Assembly. Sited upon a broad, flat plaza along the river, with the buildings of historic Manhattan as a backdrop, the new buildings — pure modernist objects — were startling.

Soon thereafter, the maverick architect-turned-president of Lever Brothers, Charles Luckman, commissioned Skidmore, Owings & Merrill's Gordon Bunshaft to design its Park Avenue headquarters. Fig. 1.20 Again, a narrow vertical tower was set on its end atop a second story horizontal slab, beneath which a kind of uninterrupted public space flowed, giving the building a floating quality. By 1958, Mies van der Rohe's Seagram Building was completed across the street. Fig. 1.21 It was an even more radical and pure departure from the historic building codes. Fully obliterating the lot-line sensibility of prior buildings, the thirty-seven-story bronze monolith sat centered at the rear of its site facing Park Avenue with a broad granite plaza surrounding it on three sides. The ground-floor lobby was recessed under the tower and fully glazed, allowing viewers to see only the travertine elevator shafts spanning floor to ceiling. The popular ascent of these three modernist buildings, among others, led to excitement both in the street

and in the profession. By 1960, the city's zoning ordinances were being rewritten to not only allow for these new aberrations but to provide density bonuses of up to twenty percent for projects composed of tall slender towers and large open plazas which would comprise a minimum of forty percent of the site area. These ordinances were ultimately imitated in other major American cities, and a new wave of modern skyscrapers issued forth. Fig. 1.22

It was only one year later, in 1961, that Jane Jacobs published *The Death and Life of Great American Cities*. Parallel to the dawning triumph of the great modern skyscraper, Jacobs and others were deeply disturbed by the effects of institutional planning and monolithic capital on the quality of life in the city. In New York City, Robert Moses' grand city projects threatened neighborhoods as large-scale commercial buildings replaced residences and introduced massive building scale as well as major transportation improvements into city streets. Tall glass extrusions began to appear in every major city, stripped by real estate developers of detail, floating in windswept and ceremonial plazas, yet fully occupied by efficient, and undiscerning, tenants. Other critiques appeared, some from professional and academic quarters, such as Robert Venturi's 1966 *Complexity and Contradiction in Architecture*. In response to a host of mounting voices, and in an attempt to further develop the building type, some high-rise architects began to experiment with more complex modern geometries while others recalled the more affable pre-war days of romantic historicism. With cities and public opinion veering to and fro, each of these trends continues to this day, personified at the opposite ends of the spectrum by the skyscraper proposals of such architects as Daniel Libeskind and Robert A. M. Stern.

By 1982 in New York, and soon thereafter in most major American cities, planning codes were once again being rewritten in support of pre-modern and now postmodern tall buildings within the city. These revisions are still largely on the books, in some cases expanded and revised, but generally reflective of institutional support for the restoration of the historic city. In the past decade, as the majority of skyscraper construction world-wide has shifted abroad, and American real estate markets have begun to associate value with the identity of prominent design architects, this model has been challenged and cities frequently find themselves speculating on the transformative powers of innovative and iconic skyscrapers that operate outside established guidelines.

Context and Consensus

Current regulation of the design and construction of tall buildings in American cities
concerns a wide range of evolving issues.
While regional differences are significant,
the public entitlement process for major
buildings is generally highly layered, assigning to project sponsors the responsibility to
address issues of an ever-growing host of
stakeholders. These normally include planning
departments with their various divisions, city
councils and building departments, but can
also engage community redevelopment
agencies, design review boards, preservation
commissions, neighborhood councils, home-
owner groups, transportation agencies, state
environmental review bodies, cultural affairs
and public arts groups, energy conservation
boards and more. Add to these the generally
high public interest in large buildings, informed by growing media coverage, and most
skyscrapers today become the product of an
intense and protracted public discussion over
appearance, function and local impacts. Some
of the recurrent themes from this discussion
today, either in the form of prescriptive
guidelines or in public debate, are as follows:

Height and Bulk

The questions of appropriate height and
overall massing of the skyscraper are always
prominent issues. Sometimes relative height
is of concern in relationship to existing
buildings, historic landmarks, the location
and degree of shade and shadow, view
corridors, or the general skyline of the city in
question. Of equal or greater concern can be
the overall massing of the tower, frequently in
the lower register of the building as it relates
to adjacent buildings. Projects in cities with
neighborhoods of relatively consistent
historic fabric, such as New York City,
Boston or San Francisco, will frequently be
required to adhere to guidelines that regulate
street-wall height and prominent setbacks
reminiscent of New York's 1916 ordinance.
Often, building designers will acknowledge
the physical characteristics of adjacent
buildings in their proposed designs in
deference to the overall physical context.

Shade and Shadow

It is common for the proponents of any
building of scale to perform detailed shade
and shadow studies both throughout the day
and over the course of the year, generally
marking solstices for high and low sun, as
well as equinoxes for middle positions in
the spring and autumn. Particular attention
is given to the effects of shadow on public
open space and recreational areas either
nearby or provided by the proposed project.
Time-of-day studies are done to understand
the relationship between outdoor programs,
such as swimming pools, outdoor cafés,
playgrounds and child-care areas, and new
shadow. Shade is considered beneficial in hot
climates while disadvantageous in moderate
or cool ones. The public reaction to these
issues is perceived differently in cities with
different climates and urban traditions. One
might expect that the introduction of a new
skyscraper into an existing dense pattern of
vertical buildings such as in New York would
be viewed differently by the public than in
temperate and mid-rise cities such as San
Jose or San Diego, where a proposed tower
will likely contribute more new shadow.

Open Space

The character and purposefulness of open
space, either provided by or adjacent to,
a proposed project is typically of equal
community concern as is that of the new
building. How will the open space be used?
Does it expand the public domain and provide for uses that are not currently provided?
Is it scaled to its function and does it receive
direct sunlight? Is it planted or hardscape?
Is it skillfully integrated into the language
of the building architecture and/or the public
right-of-way? Is it secured and does it feel
safe? And, finally, does it carry other levels
of meaning with regard to its civic purpose?
For example, is it a model of sustainability, is
it restorative or remediated, does it establish
a didactic link to the history or future of the
place, or does it open itself up to the fine arts,
performance or recreational programming?
And is it fully accessible? The somewhat
urgent nature of today's discussion regarding
meaningful open space can be understood
against the backdrop of very little, if any, open
space having been provided in the earliest
commercial skyscrapers. This discussion can
be a reaction to the abstract and sometimes
purposeless exterior space in the modern
towers of the 1950s and '60s, and to the
historically inclined and figure/ground-driven
typologies of the postmodern period.

Permeability

There is much discussion about a building's
edges as it meets the public right-of-way.
Whether it forms a street-wall consistent
with other adjacent buildings, or is articulated
in plan in some meaningful or contextually
driven way, is of common concern. For three
decades now, whether a building is historicist
or modernist, the common urban design
canon has held that a building's perimeter
should be examined with respect to what
it contributes to the public domain. This
inevitably leads to a consideration not only
of entry and access into the building's ground
floor, but of the appropriate scale and level
of detail at the base of a tall building, and the

degree of transparency or permeability the tower provides along the sidewalk. Broad undifferentiated facades are widely discouraged. This tenet, plus the tendency in some locations to include above-grade parking garages, has led to the "architecturalizing" of these otherwise banal building edges. In response to this, and in pursuit of higher densities, complex mixed-use structures frequently line residences or atypical commercial space, between the "embedded" above-grade garage and the building's property line, presenting to the street a vision of occupied space, fenestration and intimate scale.

Public Improvements
Frequently, major projects are built within a city's long-term master plan, which accounts for a series of public improvements, planned to be built out incrementally as a part of each new building project. The result may vary from a single action such as planting a tree, dedicating property to provide for street widening, or an urban design overlay that prescribes street walls, setbacks, fenestration patterns, materials and colors, primary entrance locations and conditions at street intersections, to anything else the jurisdiction in its totality has determined is in the public's best interest.

Automobile and Freight Access
As part of the larger discussion of the public right-of-way, the strategic location of automobile access points into a project, which includes parking, and the location of the inevitable building loading docks are deemed important. Both are required to be located to minimize impact on normal pedestrian flow at the public thoroughfare. Motorized entries are discouraged along major or ceremonial streets. They are generally proscribed within a certain distance of corners where pedestrian circulation crosses the street at intersections, and public agencies and building designers alike discourage them from proximity to major building entrances and public open space. All these conditions are made further complex by building uses that require curbside valet parking operations.

Sustainability and Energy Management
The concerns surrounding fossil fuels, carbon emissions and climate change are becoming so widely shared as to be increasingly codified in both municipal and corporate standards. Deciding whether a new project should be mandated to meet a specified energy standard (State energy codes, LEED, GoldStar), a credible set of integrated strategies by which a new building can be built and operated with significantly less permanent impact on natural resources, is

now becoming a common and significant part of a major building's public-approval process. Frequently, a tall building, due to its scale and embodied use of materials, energy and high technology, is considered in the public realm to be energy-intensive. The needs to respond to this perception and to curb the escalating costs of building operations are encouraging comprehensive strategies.

These recurring themes comprise, in some cases, conditions imposed on building designers, in others, the subject of public conversation and debate, and at times, a mere historic reference discarded by yet other architects who pursue a transformational agenda in the design of new skyscrapers. Despite their ubiquity, these themes are managed differently in each American city. And, while there are similarities in parts of Western Europe, they vary considerably, as they do to an even greater extent in Asia and the Middle East.

The Archetype

In addition to the evolving commercial requirements of skyscrapers and the impact of public agencies and their oversight, a number of other factors have contributed to the archetype of the inevitable skyscraper.

Examining the early history of the tall building is, at one level, to understand it as the inevitable union of the planimetric grid of the city and the three-dimensional grid of the structural frame. The trabeation of multiple floor plates set traditionally upon columns led to a century of rationalist towers. Inaki Abalos and Juan Herreros refer to these towers as "reticulated,"[10] while Rem Koolhaas terms them "Cartesian."[11] Le Corbusier's first cruciform towers set within a reinvented city plan, van der Rohe's transparent charcoal images, the pre-war American skyscraper and the modern slabs which followed, all derived much of their imagery by expressing the frame in some fashion.

The first skyscrapers, which evolved from masonry load-bearing walls to a combination of structural frames and supported walls, were designed to overcome gravity. In the range of twenty to thirty stories in height, which was common for a tall building at the end of the nineteenth century, the necessary structural analysis indicated that lateral forces (wind and earthquake) became principal factors in the building design in addition to the vertical weight of gravity. The first strategy which emerged to resist these new forces involved a strengthening of column and beam connections and the introduction of shear walls throughout the building. Stiffening, bracing or welding additional structural steel mass at the connections created, in effect, a "moment frame" which resisted overturning forces, or what is

referred to as "bending moment." Fig. 1.23
These conditions were typically fully concealed once the frame received its exterior
skin but Myron Goldsmith's 1953 master's
thesis for a theoretical concrete skyscraper
gave visible expression to this phenomenon,
ushering in decades of possibility that a
unique exoskeletal frame could become
the formal basis for a skyscraper's exterior
architecture.[12] Fig. 1.24 The intellectual basis
for this idea was philosophically shared by
Mies van der Rohe and various designers
in the offices of Skidmore, Owings & Merrill
among others. Frequently, however, the
exterior design only suggested a structural
sensibility without presenting it literally.

As skyscrapers grew into the forty- to
fifty-story range, greater lateral resistance
required more comprehensive strategies. The
most common one, introduced in the 1960s,
was a combination of moving lateral resistance to the perimeter of the building plan
by way of a dense grid of structural columns
and an interior core of shear-resisting wall
segments, or braced frames. This strategy
created a ring of sellable column-free space
around the central core, to be flexibly
planned in the case of a commercial office
building, or optimally laid out as residences
in the case of an apartment tower. Fig. 1.25
Resistance to laterally induced bending was
achieved through the multiplicity of stiffened
joints now moved to the absolute exterior
of the building perimeter. A rigid "tube" was
created, which in 1974 led to the concept
of "bundled tubes" in Bruce Graham's and
Fazlur Khan's Sears Tower, for many years,
the world's tallest building. Fig. 1.26 The
structure comprised a series of nine square
plan segments, each wrapped in a dense
moment-resisting perimeter of closely spaced
columns, each dropping off at various heights
leading to two central segments which
ascended to 110 stories. Lateral belt courses
tied the tubes together, stabilizing the tower
as it narrowed in reaching its full height.

Another strategy, which developed to
counteract the lateral force problem endemic
to the taller building, was the introduction of
triangulation. Generally, a triangulated vertical
truss was introduced into a skyscraper in
concert with a frame system, whose combined effects resolved both gravity and lateral
loads. Over decades of evolution, the vertical
truss effect has been implemented inside
the vertical core of the building to replace
shear walls, throughout the cross section
of the building, as well as outside along the
perimeter of the tower. This provided the
widest possible base to resist overturning
forces. In the latter case, triangulation has
been employed and exhibited in a wide
range of ways. most notably in SOM's 1969
John Hancock Center in Chicago. Fig. 1.27

In this case, the exterior walls of the
tower are battered to increase stability (and
accommodate variously sized floor plates),
composed of a rigid orthogonal frame, and
tied to the chords of a triangular vertical
truss. The singular diagonal motif of the
window wall and the building's dark tapered
profile combine to define its iconic identity.
Further variations on this initial theme include
SOM's Alcoa Building in San Francisco, Pei
Cobb Freed & Partners Bank of China and
Norman Foster's Hong Kong and Shanghai
Bank, wherein arrays of floors are hung from
diagonal chords, fastidiously detailed and
expressed on the exterior of the building.
More contemporary versions of triangulation
include Foster's London tower for Swiss Re,
where the triangulated structure organizes
vertical space within the interior and provides
the basis for alternating glazing systems on
the exterior. Another new variant on this
theme is the dynamically triangulated expression of OMA and Arup's highly asymmetric
CCTV tower in Beijing.

Buildings which rely hugely on the strength
of perimeter vertical truss systems have
achieved extraordinary visual effects
even without expressing these systems
as architecture. Hugh Stubbins and William
Le Messurier's 1977 Citicorp Center in
Manhattan is among them with its concealed
downward triangles terminating at the
mid-span of each elevation. A super-column
is placed there, allowing conventional corner
columns to be removed to surprising effect.
The structural work to achieve this is concealed by the repetition of tinted horizontal
ribbon windows erected outside the structure.

Finally, in pursuit of innovation, hubris and
a need to widen the base of resistance to
lateral forces acting on super-tall buildings,
even further, an additional expressive and
sometimes programmatic device has been
recently employed. Skyscrapers, such as
Cesar Pelli's 1998 twin Petronas Towers
in Kuala Lumpur, and proposals submitted
in the World Trade Center Site Competition
of 2003, involved multiple towers braced by
shared floors or bridges in the upper portion
of buildings. This provided bracing and
allowed the buildings to act as one. Fig. 1.29

Commerce and Its Effects

No one has outlined as completely as Carol
Willis in her 1995 book, *Form Follows
Finance*, the historic relationship between
the development of the American skyscraper
archetype and the commercial purpose to
which it has been put. There, the interplay
of land values, density and height are elaborated. Willis explains the relationship between
parcelization in Chicago and New York and
the creation of marketable commercial space

as well as architecture as an expression of that marketplace.

While the fundamental principle of skyscraper-as-economic-engine has not changed, a number of factors have evolved to alter its realization and physical effects on the city. As land values in major commercial centers have continued to soar, the desire for greater densities and heights has persisted, requiring significantly greater monies to finance these ever larger buildings. A current project with a construction budget approaching one billion dollars is not uncommon. Inevitably, these projects take longer to entitle and to build, requiring greater return-on-investment to cover the cost of a drawn-out and non-income bearing period of design, environmental review, approvals, construction and marketing.

Spurred on by increasing land and development costs, such projects frequently bring about super-tall structures on full city blocks with an inherently monolithic scale to an urban environment characterized by a historic grain of smaller individual structures of inherent diversity. Irrespective of detailed design strategies that attempt to "scale down" the project's appearance and the infusion of mixed-use programming, the physical effects of monolithic investment capital are significant on the character of existing urban fabric. This singular phenomenon appears to be confronting cities with the possibility of new paradigms. Some municipalities are resisting the trend altogether. Others are absorbing all the commercial opportunity they can garner at various costs, while still others are attempting to define a middle ground where the super-tall and the super-large are channeled to special locations where their impacts with regard to land use, height and bulk, shade and shadow and traffic, can be considered mediated in some fashion.

As larger funds are required to finance larger ventures, as risk is diversified, multiple investment sources are pooled. Pension funds, insurance companies, banks, real estate investment trusts, and targeted investment offerings are typical sources for this capital, which is inevitably overseen by a range of development, design and construction managers. This process of finance and oversight is further institutionalized by the fact that much of this equity is held by offshore investors.

With this as backdrop, architect Alejandro Zaera-Polo, writing in the 2007 issue of the *Harvard Design Magazine,* somewhat fatalistically outlines the process of design and production for a typical commercial skyscraper. "The typical high-rise today is designed first by well-established market ratios administered by real-estate special-

ists. Population ratios, facade-to-core depths, floor-plate sizes, planning grids, floor-to-floor heights, net-to-gross ratios, and facade ratios form the first level of constraint. Safety regulations and elevator capacities, interpreted by vertical transportation and fire consultants, add more constraints. Environmental regulations, channeled into the project through mechanical and electrical engineers, constrain the skin design to achieve certain daylight and insulation values and solar gain ratios. Finally, the local construction industry's speed and skills and the price of commodities filtered through the structural consultants or contractors determine what kind of structure, and therefore massing, the project may acquire."[13]

The process by which this complex building type is extracted from a commercial program and a multi-headed source of institutionalized capital is intricate. Nevertheless, Zaera-Polo leaves the reader with a slightly more deterministic impression of the architect's role than is actually the case. To the extent that the architect's creative power is measured by his ability to innovate at every technical or formal level in what is a broadly collaborative activity in a historic building type, his creative impact can be said to be minimal. On the other hand, to the extent that his understanding of the programmatic and formal possibilities of multiple systems is sufficiently rich, and his own image of the skyscraper is clear and compelling, we can ascribe to him an artistry that is not unlike that of an orchestra conductor, a director of film, or a dance choreographer. All rely heavily on the contributions of a diverse team. And, in some form, each must respond to the specific opportunities and constraints of his art form. The measure of a skyscraper architect's impact, then, is in the nature of the comparative model we use.

The phenomenon Zaera-Polo depicts so accurately, nevertheless, is the schism that has recently emerged in what he refers to as the "typological phylum."[14] A divergence has occurred between high-rise building designs that innovate in ways that inform the building type or "phylum," and those that are designed to some extravagantly visual effect but assert no intellectual or technical basis for advancing the building type as a whole. In an image-rich world of global marketing and highly publishable architectural design competitions, the latter category of skyscrapers has blossomed in number, producing, Zaera-Polo asserts, "weird and spectacular high-rises full of contingent gestures that fail to open the market to meaningful experimentation."[15]

This hereditary "break" between those skyscrapers which attempt the invention of a commercially derived form within a broad set of a priori constraints, and those that produce novelty over meaningful redefinition of the type follows a trend of other cultural breaks initiated in the latter part of the twentieth century. Deconstructivist revisions of language, literature and culture in many forms come to mind as does the philosophical break of Manfredo Tafuri and other western Marxists, who came to eschew actual building construction in favor of critical formal exercises and commentary. However, with unprecedented growth in tall building construction now underway, and as a supreme and ironic example of the array of cultural production currently available, the skyscraper and its critique are now both constructible.

Notes

[1] Willis, *Carol, Form Follows Finance*, op. cit., 49.

[2] Doordan, Dennis P., *Twentieth-Century Architecture*, op. cit., 22.

[3] Lampugnani, Vittorio Magnago, *Berlin Modernism and the Architecture of the Metropolis*, (Mies In Berlin, Museum of Modern Art, New York, Terence Riley and Barry Bergdoll), op. cit., 46.

[4] ibid., 47.

[5] ibid., 47.

[6] ibid., 49.

[7] ibid., 43.

[8] ibid., 44.

[9] Koolhaas, Rem, *Delirious New York*, op. cit., 208.

[10] Abalos, Inaki & Herreros, Juan, *Tower and Office, From Modernist Theory to Contemporary Practice*, op. cit., 41.

[11] Koolhaas, Rem, *Delirious New York*, op. cit., 211.

[12] Abalos, Inaki & Herreros, Juan, *Tower and Office, From Modernist Theory to Contemporary Practice*, op. cit., 51.

[13] Zaera-Polo, Alejandro, *High-Rise Phylum 2007* (Harvard Design Magazine, Spring/Summer 2007), op. cit., 16.

[14] ibid., 15.

[15] ibid., 18.

Fig. 1.1 South Dearborn Street near Van Buren, looking north from right to left, Manhattan Building, 1891, Old Colony Building, 1894 and Fuller Building, 1896, Chicago. Architects from right to left: William Le Baron Jenney, Holabird and Roche, Daniel Hudson Burnham.

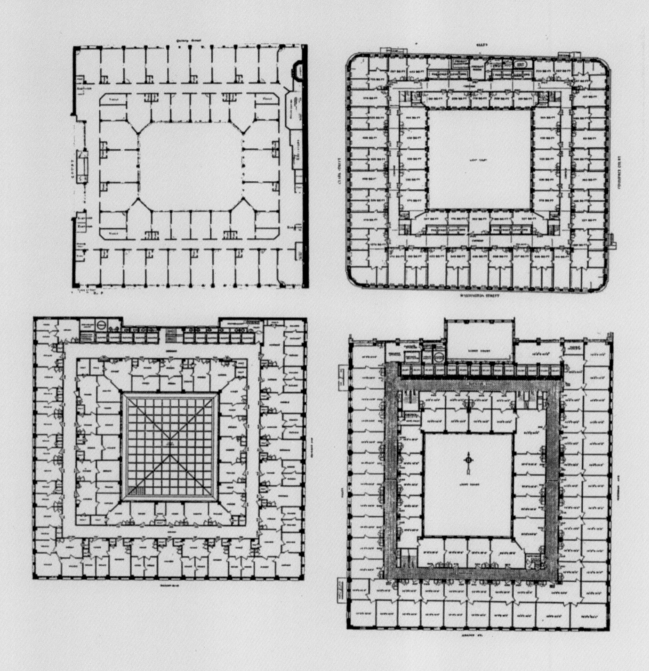

Fig. 1.2 Plans – Clockwise from top left: Rand-MacNally
Building, 1890; Conway Building, 1915; Peoples Gas Company
Building, 1911; Railway Exchange Building, 1915.

Fig. 1.3 Manhattan skyline: South Street and Jones Lane, New York City, 1936.

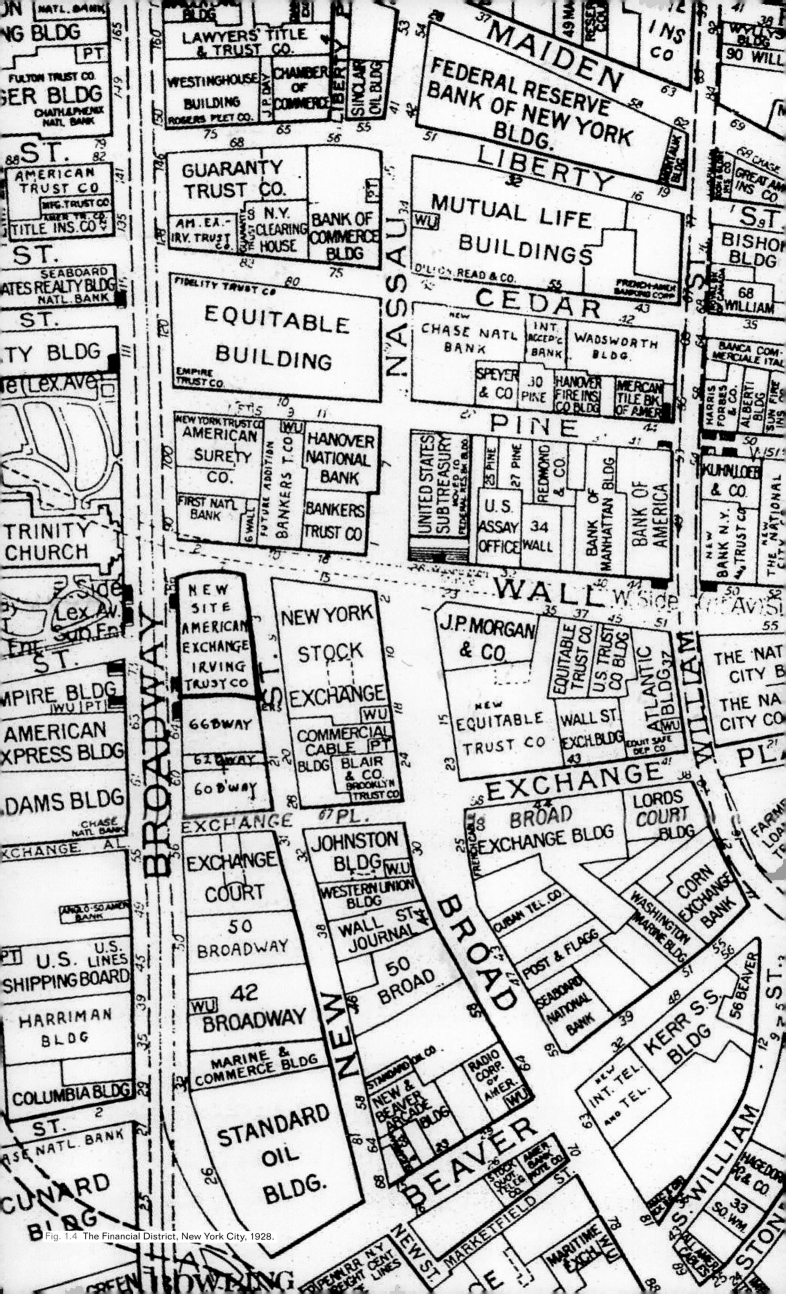
Fig. 1.4 The Financial District, New York City, 1928.

Fig. 1.5 Wainwright Building, St. Louis, 1891. Adler and Sullivan.

34

Fig. 1.6 The Equitable Building, New York City, 1915.
Ernest Graham/Graham, Anderson, Probst & White.

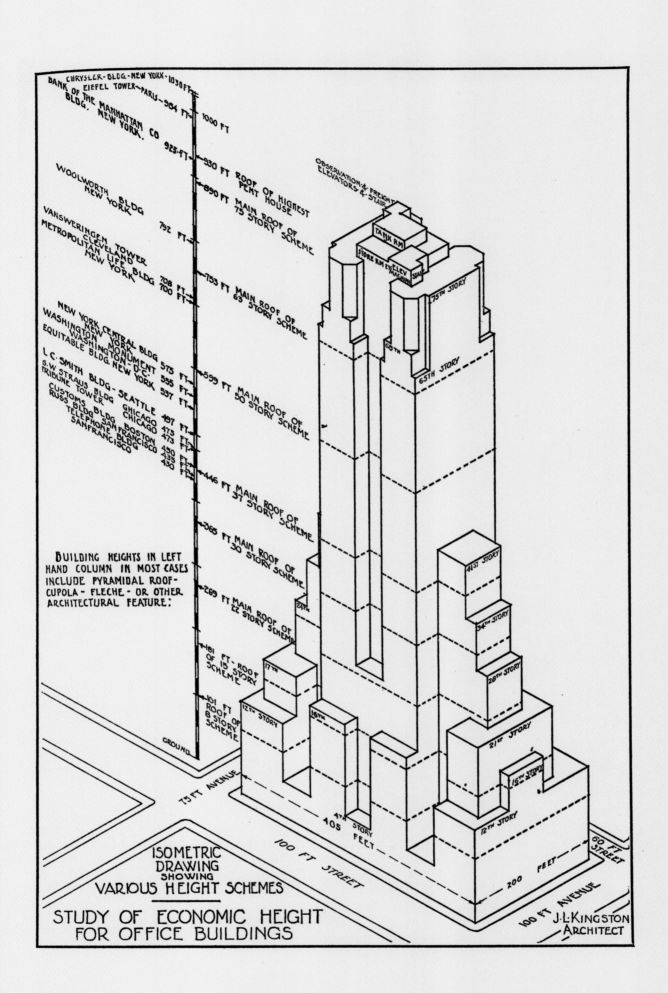

Fig. 1.7 Study of Economic Height for Office Buildings, 1930. W. C. Clark/S. W. Straus and J. L. Kingston/ Sloan and Robertson.

Fig. 1.8 Building Envelopes, 1922. Hugh Ferriss.

Fig. 1.9 Chicago Tribune Building, Chicago, 1921.
Raymond Hood/Hood & Howells.

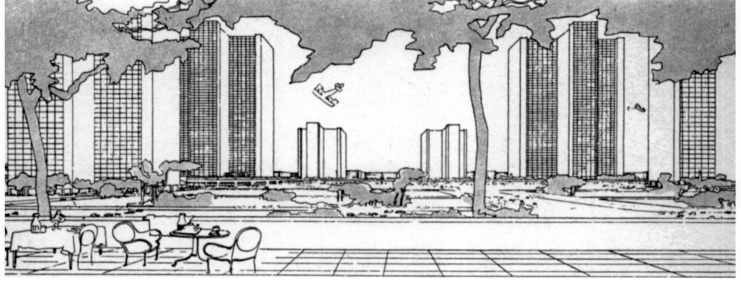

Fig. 1.10 Plan Voisin, Paris, 1925. Le Corbusier.
Fig. 1.11 A Contemporary City for Three Million, Paris, 1922. Le Corbusier.

Fig. 1.12 **The Cartesian Skyscraper, 1938. Le Corbusier.**

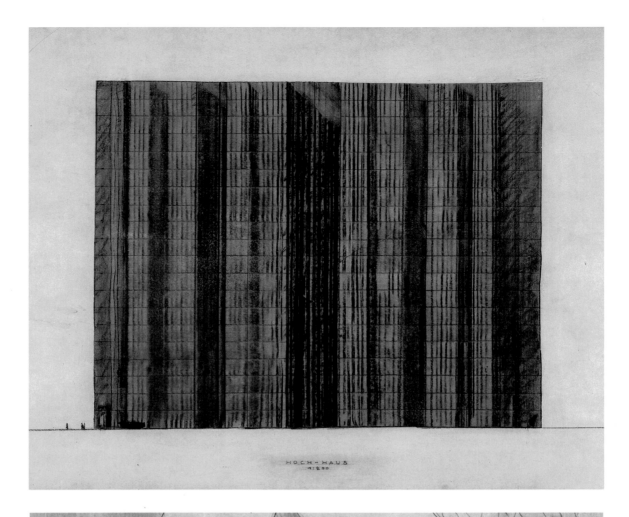

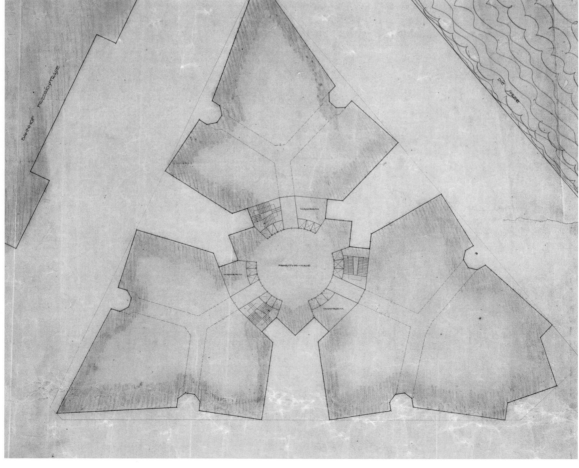

Fig. 1.13 & Fig. 1.14 Friedrichstrasse Skyscraper proposal,
Berlin, 1921. Ludwig Mies van der Rohe.

Fig. 1.15 Friedrichstrasse Skyscraper proposal.
Ludwig Mies van der Rohe.

42

Fig. 1.16 Glass Skyscraper, Berlin, 1922.
Ludwig Mies van der Rohe.

Fig. 1.17 Glass Skyscraper, elevation. Ludwig Mies van der Rohe.

Fig. 1.18 The Look Building at 488 Madison Avenue, New York City, 1950. Emery Roth and Sons.

Fig. 1.19 The United Nations, New York City, 1950. International Architecture Committee under Wallace K. Harrison.

Fig. 1.20 Lever House, New York City, 1952.
Gordon Bunshaft/Skidmore, Owings & Merrill.

Fig. 1.21 The Seagram Building, New York City, 1958.
Ludwig Mies van der Rohe in association with Philip Johnson.

48

Fig. 1.22 Sixth Avenue, New York City, 1970.

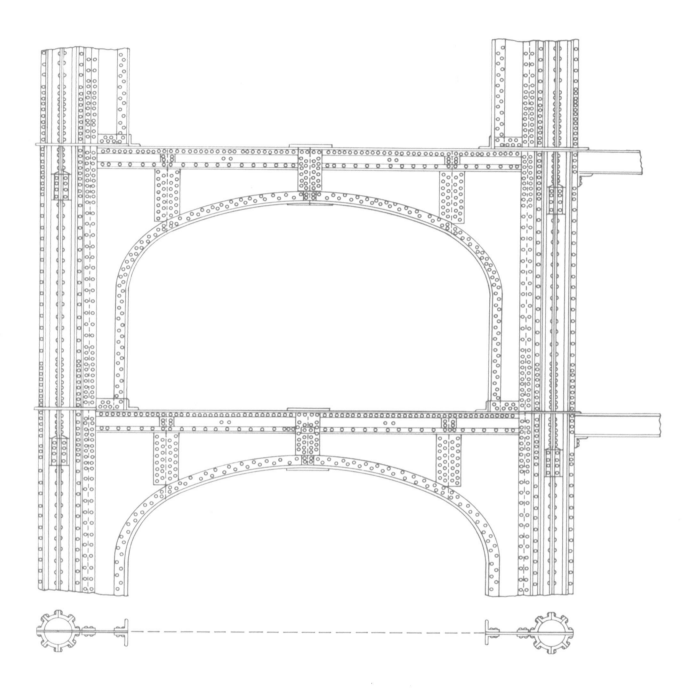

Fig. 1.23 **Old Colony Building, Chicago, 1894. Holabird and Roche.**

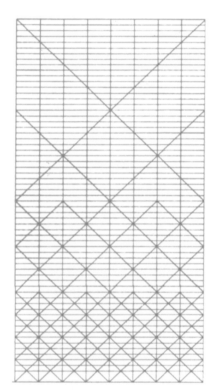
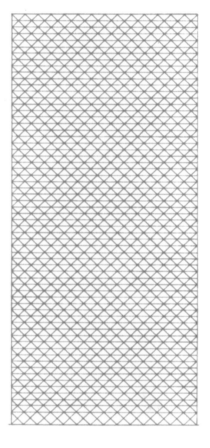
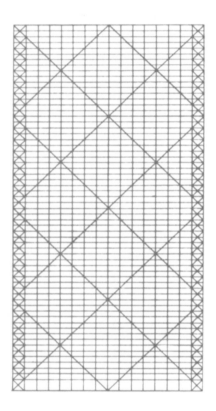

Fig. 1.24 Cross-braced steel variations on the concrete
skyscraper, 1953. Myron Goldsmith.

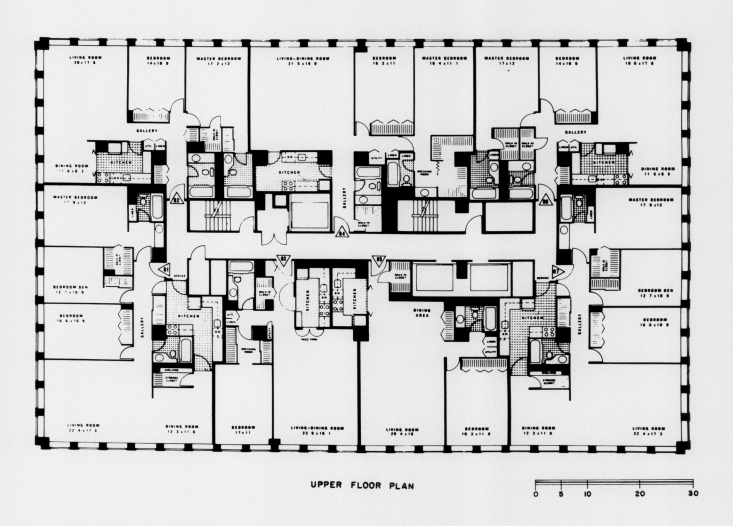

UPPER FLOOR PLAN

0 5 10 20 30

Fig. 1.25 Chestnut-Dewitt Apartments, Chicago, 1965.
Skidmore, Owings & Merrill.

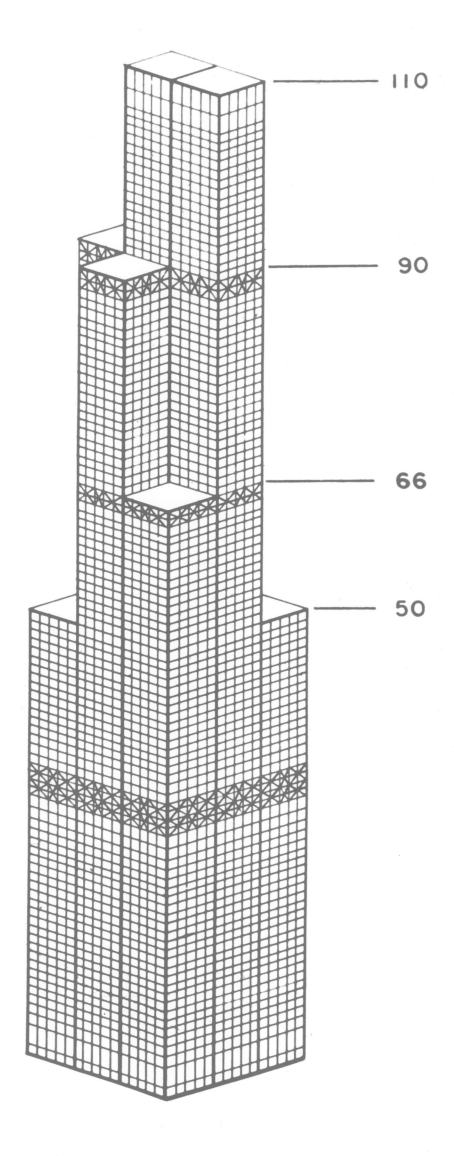

110

90

66

50

Fig. 1.26 **Sears Tower, Chicago, 1974. Skidmore, Owings & Merrill.**

Fig. 1.27 John Hancock Center, Chicago, 1969.
Skidmore, Owings & Merrill.

Fig. 1.28 Citicorp Building, New York City, 1977.
Hugh Stubbins and Associates.

Fig. 1.29 World Trade Center proposal, 2002. Collaboration between: RUR, FOA, UNStudio, Kevin Kennon, Greg Lynn FORM and Imaginary Forces.

Chapter 2

The Enrichment of Vertical Space

Inevitable Skyscraper

Trajectories

Mixed-use skyscrapers in the West have struggled to gain traction. Historically, the skyscraper has been a vertical extrusion of similarly inhabited floors. Implicit in the concept of tall is the omnipresence of gravity as both a structural force as well as a force to be overcome to achieve accessibility. While horizontal space symbolizes a kind of sociable and barrier-free access, vertically organized space typically presents obstacles to movement and visibility, separating activity on one floor from the next. Horizontal space is epitomized as flexibility, organizable into shades of public, semi-private and private, while a vertical extrusion of similar floor plates implies privacy and separation. Perhaps not enough volumetrically rich buildings have been designed and built for the public to think otherwise. From a builder's perspective, it has generally been easier and less costly to construct a single use over many nearly identical floors than to stack multiple uses vertically. Each functional layer carries with it a unique set of engineering, circulation and programmatic requirements, which inevitably need to be coordinated over the height of the building with other functional layers and their required systems.

This stacking calls for the optimization of systems competing to satisfy different goals on different floors and the resulting redundancies in building systems add to the overall cost of the tall building.

From its inception, there has been, in the public imagination at least, a vision that the mixed-use skyscraper could overcome the banal repetition of floors that characterizes so many commercial high-rise buildings. Even nineteenth and early twentieth century office towers frequently had multi-story lobbies with ground-floor retail and mezzanines, rooftop amenities and setbacks, and light courts, which created opportunity for usable outdoor space. Apartment towers and hotel buildings fared better as they inevitably carried with them more and varied amenities to support the residences and guestrooms. Increasing density, greater building height, and mixed-use zoning in the central city fired the public imagination for the multi-layered, multi-use vertical city long before it became common in actual skyscrapers. Both Chicago and New York City, with their distinctive range of building types and sizes, their elevated subways, highways, bridges and pedestrian crossovers, became the inspiration for visions of mixed-use vertical living created by artists and designers worldwide. These early visions anticipated the realities that would come later.

At the turn of the twentieth century, guidebook publisher Moses King's picture postcards of a recognizable yet visionary Manhattan absorbed the idea of multi-layered buildings, like Grand Central Station with its rich section of public and private spaces, concourses and platforms, and extrapolated them into dense multilayered images of a three-dimensional and vertically accessible cluster of skyscrapers.[1] Fig. 2.1 Throughout Europe, architects such as Le Corbusier, August Perret and André Lurçat in France, and Ludwig Hilberseimer, Mies van der Rohe and Walter Gropius in Germany, were increasingly focused on the implications of tall buildings within the context of an industrializing and dense city. Nevertheless, New York City stood out worldwide as the pre-eminent symbol of an actual skyscraper city with its vertiginous heights and its layered mixture of uses. In Italy, the writings of Mario Morasso (*Artistic Imperialism*, 1903 and *The New Mechanical Aspect of the World,* 1907), the theories of Filippo Tommaso Marinetti, and the proposals of the young architect Antonio Sant'Elia were highly influenced by the visuality of rich, industrial and vertical cities like New York. *The Future Circulation and the Skyscrapers of New York* and similar drawings frequently appeared in Italian books and magazines.[2] (*L'Illustrazione Italiana,* 1913). Fig. 2.2

Between 1912 and 1914, two of France's leading Art Nouveau architects, Henri Sauvage and Charles Sarazin designed and built a pioneering stepped apartment building on Paris' Rue Vavin known as the Athletic House with Terraces. Fig. 2.4 – Fig. 2.5 This remarkable building both redefined the traditional tall (seven to ten stories) building's relationship to the Parisian city street as well as redistributed the building's volume in a way that created an interior ground-level atrium. Linear terraces appeared atop multiple building setbacks, establishing generous and highly usable "outdoor rooms."

By 1914, the avant-garde architect Antonio Sant'Elia was publishing his *Manifesto of Futurist Architecture,* illustrated with drawings for a new machine-age world-city, La Citta Nuova (The New City). In the same year, Sant'Elia produced drawings for a proposed glass-and-steel terraced apartment building, which appeared to inherit qualities from both the public images of urban New York as well as the typological innovations of the Parisian stepped apartment block. Fig. 2.6 As the apartment building at this time was among the tallest of urban structures in cities like Paris and Milan, and it made up the predominant fabric of these and other European cities, Sant'Elia's drawings were archetypal as well as innovative and elegant. The ground floor was designed to support the commercial street with sidewalk-focused uses, while linear terraces above were set back, looking down into the public right of way. Large glazed window panels infill the primary structure while a tall vertical recess in the side of the tower suggests light into a multi-storied interior atrium. The elevator is pulled out of the mass of the building and articulated as a slim free-standing tower with arched bridges leading back to the receding mass of the apartment block behind. The top of the building displays a kind of ad hoc mechanical silhouette characteristic of modern industrial structures. No detailed plans have been found for Sant'Elia's powerful image, but the programmatic and formal elements expressed in his perspective drawing are features today's architects still refer to with interest.

Literary and cinematic representations of the skyscraper in the modern multi-layered city began to come forward at about the same time. Notably, the architecturally trained German director, Fritz Lang, created *Metropolis,* a 1927 film based on Thea von Harbou's book of the same name. Magnificently illustrated by set designer Erich Kettelhut, the illustrations and sets portray a vertiginous and dark city of the future, one of enormous density and verticality, with its elevated transportation systems and little recognition of nature. Fig. 2.3 Subsequently, iconic films, such as William Cameron Menzies' *Things to Come* (1936),

King Vidor's *The Fountainhead* (1949), Jacques Tati's *Playtime* (1967), and Ridley Scott's *Blade Runner* (1982), have continued to propel the popular image of the multi-use skyscraper environment.

Amusement parks and expositions were often historic catalysts for imagining tall buildings and the pictorial possibilities for large ensembles of towers. The 1889 World Exposition in Paris, and its building of the Eiffel Tower, succeeded in initiating the kind of schizophrenic public dialogue that surrounds tall buildings to this day — wonderment and admiration on the one hand for the achievement of height, and resistance to the technological character and alien scale on the other. In his widely read *Delirious New York*, Rem Koolhaas described Frederic Thompson, an architectural drop-out and entrepreneur, imagining and building Coney Island's Luna Park in 1903 as the "first city of towers." Vertical sunlit confections by day, the towers sported newly available strings of electric lights which transformed the towers to radiance by night. These images, in situ and on postcards, were among the first to exhibit the kind of nocturnal magic of modern towers after dark. Fig. 2.7

But as real skyscrapers broke free from single-use formulas or transformed themselves into something fundamentally unique, developers and architects began in the first part of the century to envision vertical buildings with multiple uses. Typical of the earliest proposals was developer Theodore Starrett's 1906 plan for a one-hundred-story building for New York City. Fig. 2.8 Fantastic, if only for its height, the massive tower would include "industry at the bottom, business in the next section, residences above, and a hotel above that, with each section separated by public plazas including theaters, shopping districts, and, at the top, an amusement park, roof garden, and swimming pool."[3] While detailed plans for such a building were never made available, and Starrett's scheme remained unbuilt, such a vertical distribution of uses, although extravagant in its day, would not be completely foreign a century later in highly dense Asian cities or in ambitious schemes within dense high-value Western cities. In fact, much architectural and urban planning theory today is focused on differentiating various levels of tall buildings physically, as well as energizing the city at all hours of the day and night. Interdependent uses have been cited to help provide "eyes on the street," reduce dependence on transit, and support a longer retail day, boosting the commercial value of urban real estate. Retail and live-work opportunities are frequently identified at the ground level with commercial office uses or a profusion of hotel products with serviced condominium residences above that. As tall buildings become denser, designers look to locating a range of social and recreational spaces within the property as well, whether in basements, at ground-floor mezzanine levels, on roof decks or as distinguishing features within the body of the tall building.

Though New York City eventually captured the lead in the number and variety of mixed-use tall buildings in America, one of the first fully developed and robustly programmed of these was the 1889 Auditorium Building by Adler & Sullivan in Chicago. Fig. 2.9 Designed to include a 4,000-seat concert hall (1,200 more seats than its competitor, New York's Metropolitan Opera House), the overall building was the largest private project of its day. The massive ten-story building contained a decorative elevator and water-storage tower above, and in its base was located the concert hall, commercial offices and retail, a hotel of 400 luxurious guest suites, plus banqueting facilities.[4] While the building was tall in its time, it contained Chicago's characteristically broad floor plate and resembled more a horizontal mass with a tower outcropping, than what came to be known within the next three decades as a proper skyscraper.

Similarly, although New York City's first Waldorf Astoria Hotel of 1893 was only thirteen stories tall, its alignment of windows and its rooftop towers and turrets suggested aspirations of verticality. Relocated to Park Avenue in 1924 and significantly redesigned by architects Schultze & Weaver, the new building assumed the form of a highly modified skyscraper in order to both incorporate the wide array of services and interior spatial types required of a world-class hotel of its day, and to assume the cachet associated with being a modern skyscraper. Fig. 2.10 This was no easy task for the designers, as the massing for a hotel with long corridors and maximum guestrooms per floor resulted in a wide, low podium with multiple hotel wings rising into a broad U-shaped slab. To bring such a wide mass into the shape of a vertical skyscraper, the building's corners were cut away, creating strong vertical lines at the building's edges; windows and pilasters were vertically aligned; and the two "corners" of the U plan were stepped back at the top to be crowned by two identical vertically expressed cupolas. The wide building slab had been inventively transformed and detailed into the lightness of two adjacent skyscrapers ascending between two lower towers. The perceptual battle had been won. And it was clear now that to be important, a building needed to be not only tall, but seen as the image of a skyscraper as well.

The Waldorf Astoria, which is still with us today, maintains its primary support spaces in the three levels of basement, while a shallow ground floor accommodates an array of shops, customer services, and food and beverage establishments. Principal grade-level entrances are located on all four sides of the block, while several multi-story floors above create a podium base and include lobbies, banqueting spaces and service mezzanines. Their exposed roofs double as outdoor courtyards for relaxation and food and beverage service. Above the courtyards are fifteen massive guestroom floors in the form of four vertical slabs, the outer two of which drop off and are topped by two extraordinary entertainment lounges open to city views. The two central slabs then are set back and continue upward to the top of the building comprised of hotel suites and a double-height penthouse floor. The new Waldorf Astoria provided a conceptual model for the marriage of post-1916 building form in New York City and an energetically mixed-use program that mirrored the city at large.

Shortly thereafter, Starrett & Van Vleck's 1931 design for the Downtown Athletic Club represented a more subdued extrusion of varying spaces in the conventional stepped tower of the day. Fig. 2.11 A publicly accessible three-story podium connected it to the street and to the smaller buildings in the neighborhood of the time. A vertical stack of varying floor-to-floor heights accommodated a wide range of recreational and athletic spaces above, concealed within an unexpressive exterior, inclined toward the vertical. Several mid-rise setbacks then gave way to twenty narrow guestroom floors above. As in the case of the Waldorf, architectural design efforts appear to have emphasized unity and verticality in the massing, cladding and exterior expression of the vertically diverse program.

More than any project of its day, the design of New York's Rockefeller Center symbolized the realities of America's commercial real estate market, of which the skyscraper was the prime signifier, and the urban theories of a nascent European modernism. Built on three blocks of Midtown Manhattan, the project encompassed fifteen acres, and to this day, is a benchmark in the legacy of three-dimensional urbanism. Beginning in 1926, as a site search for a new Metropolitan Opera house, various locations in midtown Manhattan were examined until a three-block site between Fifth and Sixth Avenues and Forty-Eighth and Fifty-First Streets, owned by Columbia University, was identified as being the most advantageous. John D. Rockefeller, the industrialist and philanthropist, agreed to assume responsibility for the project, imagining a kind of world-class "Rockefeller City." It would be multi-use, self-sufficient

and exemplary. Because of his own lack of training in matters of real estate development, he delegated business matters to an associate, John Todd. In 1928, he created the Metropolitan Square Corporation whose mission was to develop the property. Over the early course of examining alternative schemes for the site, a notable group of architects was assembled under the banner of Associated Architects. They included Wallace K. Harrison, J.O. Brown, Henry Hofmeister, Hugh Robertson, Andrew Reinhard, Harvey Wiley Corbett and Raymond Hood. While architectural studies proceeded in a team format, it appears that Hood led the design effort, renowned as he was for having won the Chicago Tribune Tower competition, designing the American Radiator Building at Bryant Park, and having studied the tall building type for more than a decade.

During the course of the project, many influential events occurred that materially affected the ultimate design of the buildings. At the outset, The Metropolitan Opera Company withdrew its participation and in 1929, the American stock market crashed. Rockefeller, nevertheless, decided to retain control of the land and continue with the project. Multiple and disparate schemes began to emerge from the joint office of Associated Architects that developed each of the blocks as if they were separate properties, each meeting the design guidelines of the 1916 zoning ordinance in different ways: Some featured three-stepped podia and three narrow tower slabs, some boasted paired towers, while others appeared with a taller tower in the central block, initially up against Fifth Avenue and, alternatively, to the rear at Sixth. Additional proposals lifted the primary pedestrian circulation zone above the street level, creating major plazas above the dense street-level traffic. Schemes emerged that connected the tops of the mid-height podiums with horizontal bridges. Hood even introduced a scheme that attempted to treat the three blocks as a single superblock with four stepped towers facing each other in the center of the project area as a pyramid. Fig. 2.12 – Fig. 2.15 After much debate, the committee embraced a diagram that allowed all streets to run through the project area, located the dominant Radio Corporation of America (RCA) Building to the center-rear with lower podiums fronting onto Fifth Avenue, four towers of lesser height spread out to the corners of the property, and a large depressed plaza to the east of the RCA entrance. The sunken plaza was initially planned as an entry to the subway system below but ultimately was developed as an ice rink and social space. Fig. 2.16

The importance of Rockefeller Center as a model cannot be overstated. Influenced by

European architects who drew up proposals for tall towers within their cities but had no opportunity to build them, many of the Center's elements incorporated theoretical concepts into the project. The highly landscaped rooftops at all levels were reminiscent of Le Corbusier's rooftop proposals, brought to further fruition years later in his designs for the Unité apartment towers. Upper level pedestrian bridges, although later dropped from the construction, as well as the multitude of grade and below-grade circulation levels, resonated with Hilberseimer's proposals for Vertical City and Sant'Elia's Citta Nuova. The rich variety of mixed-use programming at the ground level of the property spoke to both Hilberseimer's, and later, Team Ten's admonition to avoid the isolation of Le Corbusier's initial tower proposals and provide mixed-use elements within walking distance at the base of urban buildings. Finally, while the architecture of the complex retained its distinctly Manhattan profile and its romanticized limestone exterior, the stark geometry of its stepped massing, its vertical fenestration, and its flat building tops reference the modernist architecture of the moment.

Visits to New York in the 1930s by architects such as Le Corbusier, Walter Gropius and Mies van der Rohe, allowed them to view the effects of density and congestion, the utility of highly urbanized open space, and elaborations on the idea of the tower conceived as a monumental and sculpted solid rather than a glazed extrusion of identical floor plates. The opportunism and flexibility with which Rockefeller Center's edges incorporated and acknowledged the buildings and street patterns around them characterized the skyscraper as mediator, not just purifier. The enormous project stood as a model for the dialectics of abstraction and context, modernity and history, uniqueness and familiarity. Furthermore, the final building design emerged from the dynamics of a culturally unified committee rather than from the mind of a single heroic innovator. The project was complex, democratic and characteristically American. Completed in 1940, a decade after the Great Depression began and a year before the start of World War II, Rockefeller Center opened as the last of the pre-war skyscrapers.

Le Corbusier's visit to New York had both intrigued him and made him contemptuous of the American city. Much taken by Manhattan's density and its apparent verticality when viewed from the sea, he deplored what he considered the irrational variety and lack of aestheticism that characterized the urban architecture. He had traveled widely and executed a number of modestly scaled projects since his grand proposals of the 1920s. He had been invited to prepare large-scale proposals throughout South America, North Africa and Europe, but none had been realized. Fig. 2.17 In 1945, following World War II, he was invited by Claudius Petit, France's minister of reconstruction, to design and build five apartment blocks throughout the country, each sized to house a different number of families. Given a relatively free hand, and the ability to waive all building regulations, many of Le Corbusier's theories of the city and vertical living from the prior two decades reappeared in the design of these apartment blocks, the first of which was Marseilles' Unité d'Habitation, designed to accommodate 1,500 residents. Fig. 2.18 Now, with no commission to design the larger land plan, and in the wake of various international critiques to his city plans of the '20s, Le Corbusier cleverly folded his city ideas into the building, including as much of his earlier "Five Points of the New Architecture" as was applicable, and simultaneously incorporating diverse program elements into the single tall building. Fig. 2.22 The tower became the city. The new reinforced concrete, vertically mixed-use Unité d'Habitation, completed in 1952, could not have appeared more different from those cruciform glass towers of 1922.

With the consolidation of so many ideas into a single building, the Unité had a rich and radical appearance. Applying lessons learned from his residential work with villas and studios, Le Corbusier created vertical duplexes which maximized natural light and alternating corridors at every third floor which became more populated and sociable. Fig. 2.19 – Fig. 2.21 Outdoor terraces adjoined living rooms and were bordered by a bris-soleil to encourage natural ventilation yet provide shade. A shopping street was inserted midheight in the building slab, a feature that proved to be under-utilized and was relocated in subsequent projects to the ground floor. The building mass was lifted off the ground plane so that landscape, view and accessibility could pass beneath, a gesture to the architect's idealized, yet vanished, ground plane. And, finally, the roof deck became a highly articulated surface, with the integration of building shafts and generous recreational and landscaped terraces. As steel had become significantly more expensive following the war effort, Le Corbusier designed the entire building in unfinished cast-in-place reinforced concrete with the application of bright colors. For Le Corbusier, thirty years of theory and practice were brought together in the five Unité projects.

With the devastation of major European cities during World War II, the ongoing modernist critique moved to take on the challenge of rebuilding the city and judged the performance of individual buildings in relation to their role in the overall city plan. With large areas of destruction, opportunities suddenly appeared for rethinking major segments of the urban landscape, and the large scale and idealism of the '20s returned to the concerns of architecture. The work of Team Ten, particularly the drawings of Cluster City, designed in 1952 by its chief proponents, Alison and Peter Smithson, supported the idea of self-sufficient residential and commercial elements assembled around multipurpose structures which themselves were clustered around transportation networks. Jose Luis Sert, who served as both dean of Harvard's Graduate School of Design and president of Congrès Internationaux d'Architecture Moderne (CIAM), convened the first Urban Design Symposium in 1956. Shortly thereafter, Harvard initiated the first urban design program in an architectural school. Sert recognized that the larger mixed-use issues of cities constituted the real program for relevant modern buildings and he was offering an alternative to the expanding two-dimensional planning culture which was multiplying to address the problems of the city. The seriousness and scope of such work, he believed, deserved the architect's attention. In a burst of enthusiasm for the prospect of entirely remaking the historic city, so-called "mat" buildings, such as the Free University in Berlin by Candilis-Josic-Woods with Manfred Schiedhelm in 1963, and buildings by Aldo Van Eyck and other Europeans, led to a body of work the author Reyner Banham referred to as "mega-structures." Incrementalism reigned supreme in North America with mega-structures a topic for theorists and academics, and affecting practice on the fringe with "systems analysis", such as Ezra Ehrenkrantz's universal Schools Construction System Development (SCSD) and Moshe Safdie's Habitat. Architects in Japan spun the concept off into a building-oriented Metabolism, which produced a few extraordinary and idiosyncratic towers, but generally more proposals than buildings.

The prospect that the building could be the city caused many Western architects to aspire to a mixed-use skyscraper of the future. Prevailing modernist preferences resulted in singular and iconic buildings which downplayed the expression of mixed-use elements integral to their conception. Frank Lloyd Wright's 1950 Johnson Wax Research Tower and his nineteen-story Price Tower in Bartlesville, Oklahoma of 1956, in which each floor was composed of one quarter residence and three quarters office, took their architectural cues from the aesthetics of the buildings' structures. Fig. 2.23 – Fig. 2.24 When, in the same year, Wright proposed the One-Mile-High Skyscraper as a vertical focal point

for his vision of Broadacre City, the concept was said to contain multiple uses: including office space, residences and services. Fig. 2.25 The building's elevations displayed no expression of this inherent variety, instead opting for a slim trapezoidal mass receding evenly to its pointed top. The skyscraper was represented to sit on a broad flat plain, the modernist object divorced from any integration with other uses populating that plain. The 500-story tower was in fact, as Wright called it, a "tree that escaped the forest." The One-Mile-High Skyscraper, in concept and form, prefigured a series of proposals that would follow much later, such as Norman Foster's 1989 Millennium Tower for Tokyo Bay Fig. 2.26 and Renzo Piano's London Bridge Tower, scheduled to be completed in 2009.

Foster's proposal for the Millennium Tower stood 840 meters high at 170-stories, twice the size of the Sears Tower in Chicago. Rising two kilometers offshore in Tokyo Bay, the skyscraper comprised a vertical neighborhood, similar in size to the entire nearby Ginza ward, and including office space, hotels, shops and residential apartments. Principal vertical circulation was planned to utilize a "metro" of super-sized elevators carrying 160 persons each. These would stop at platforms every thirty stories. Visitors would complete their journey in high-speed local elevators serving each floor.

In the built world of modern mixed-use towers, which began in earnest in the 1960s, SOM's John Hancock Center in Chicago followed the theoretical modernist tendency to visually incorporate its programmatic diversity into one unitary and minimally differentiated mass. Bottom to top: retail, commercial office, recreational, residential, restaurant/observation level, telecommunications platform, all uses were enclosed in a tapering rectangular volume and wrapped in an exterior triangulated structure. Thirty years later, SOM reprised the mixed-use concept in 2004 with Time Warner Center in New York City, a twin-tower scheme of office, retail, condominiums, hotel, theater and parking. It was developed by The Related Companies and financed by Apollo Real Estate Advisors with what is believed to be the largest construction loan in United States history. A second archetype of mixed-use vertical buildings emerged in the 1970s, with Chicago's Water Tower Place and the evolution of a series of projects by architect/developer John Portman following his Peachtree Center in Atlanta. These buildings comprised a skyscraper of generally singular use, usually office or hotel set upon a multi-level podium that contained retail services, food, cinema, banqueting in the case of a hotel, and, in some projects, a destination shopping center. Such buildings generally incorporated tall atriums to maximize visibility and way-finding, were frequently skylit to illuminate circulation and common space, and, in some cases, accommodated above-grade pedestrian connections to adjacent parcels within the city.

Radical Invention

The neo-avant-garde voices in architecture emerging in the late 1950s and well into the 60s, began reacting to the realities of post-war Europe, in their view, the somewhat universal and staggeringly mundane build-out of so many European cities following the war. Spiritless, rectangular slab after slab was being installed throughout Europe and the United Kingdom until a movement like the New Brutalism could adapt modernism's means and methods to parody the objects of its own contempt. In this moment, situationist artists and cultural critics moved into the fray with discourse aimed at both reanimating the city as well as chiding the positivist objectivity which the early modernist proposals had promised, and on which actual modern buildings were failing to deliver. The work of these architects and critics, England's Archigram preeminent among them, focused on visually lavish proposals incorporating pop iconography, futurism and the concept of the building, in all its diverse and expressive contents, as a microcosm of the city. Fig. 2.27 – 2.28 Peter Cook, a principal and founder of the group was quoted at the time as saying, "People draw a big distinction between projects and buildings but I don't. A lot of our projects are highly serious and a lot of built buildings are a sort of bad joke."[5]

Highly visible from the period are the Archigram images from Ron Herron's Walking City proposal of 1964. These drawings depict an uncertain world swimming in advanced technology, constantly changing and humorous. A peaceful detente appears to have been reached between the staid cityscape of the past and the vacillating and connective agglomerations of the future. The new architecture is mechanically rendered yet biomorphic. It opportunistically consumes underutilized space, be it the Hudson River or an infill site, laminating itself to existing buildings or transportation networks, and moving on.

As visually arresting as Walking City was, the proposal which brought together all of Archigram's persistent themes was Peter Cook's Plug-In City. While highly conceptual, the scope of Plug-In City gives us an indication of the breadth of the group's critique and its intellectual ambition. Technological and ad hoc, its contents are interchangeable, its boundaries shifting. Plug-In City carried

with it the animation and pure pleasure of defying the high modernist commercial orthodoxies of the day. De-emphasizing the monumentality generally associated with mega-structures, Plug-In City was purely provisional, projecting a sense that important elements were always being added as others were being subtracted. As the architecture embraced change, so the building and the city united in a fit of continual regeneration.

In recent years, artists and architects have struggled with the inherent constraints of linearity and redundancy in the tall-building type. Symbolized by Isamu Noguchi's Energy Void of 1971, the desire to turn a linear form in on itself is one not foreign to architects struggling to identify new volumetric, programmatic and circulatory possibilities within the building and has led to a rethinking of the formal structure of the skyscraper. Fig. 2.30 Theoretical until recently, this concept now speaks to unique possibilities for tall mixed-use buildings.

Peter Eisenman's 1992 proposal for the Max Reinhardt Haus, to be located in Berlin on the site of Hans Poelzig's former Schauspielhaus, represents a first adaptation of this notion to architecture. Fig. 2.31 – Fig. 2.32 Rising above the surrounding skyline, Eisenman's tower is a series of continuous folding triangular planes which comprise a "heterotopia that includes a complete range of contemporary activities for body and mind, including a hotel, beauty and fitness establishments, commercial office space, a sports and game center, film and video auditoria, press agencies, restaurants, and video- and audiotheques."[6] As the two vertical shafts rise they become independent floor plates, one comprising the hotel floors, while the other constitutes the office floors, joining at the top for specialized assembly areas with highly articulated ceilings. The proposal is an interesting one and tests the degree of fit between a preordained formal concept and the public/private opportunities available within a generalized mixed-use skyscraper program.

Eisenman's unbuilt project was notably retrieved a decade later by Rem Koolhaas and Office for Metropolitan Architecture (OMA) through a series of projects culminating in Central Chinese Television Headquarters (CCTV) for Beijing. Fig. 2.33 – Fig. 2.34 Koolhaas' own parallel interest in deconstructing the limitations of verticality in the tall building can be traced to his early projects, the City Hall at The Hague (1986), the Sea Trade Center in Zeebrugge (1989), Fig. 2.35 Euralille (1988-94), to the ramped and stacked boxes of his more recent Seattle Public Library (2004). In the CCTV building, Koolhaas' characteristic obsession with programmatic differentiation and his attraction to formal eccentricity yields a building where both tendencies are in service to a radical reworking of the archetypal skyscraper. According to OMA, the large lateral floors, and the horizontal connectivity they imply, support an interdependent loop between media production and news dissemination. Production, business and international media spaces are conceived to be codependent and not hierarchical. Heating, ventilating and cooling systems are said to thread both vertically and horizontally through the building, while sequential banks of elevators are offset as they climb the sloping shafts of the building. As the mass of the tower is deeply cantilevered, so the primary structural system is extremely non-standard. The envelope has been analyzed for variation in stresses and the triangulated structure at the building's perimeter reflects the pattern of those stresses.

Ground Zero

The world watched in 2002 and 2003 as the competition process for Lower Manhattan's Ground Zero foundered step after step, but one of its most helpful attributes has been the almost limitless exploration of skyscraper typologies proposed in both the official and unofficial presentations. Officially, seven teams presented nine proposals to the Lower Manhattan Development Corporation, among which several had much to say about mixed-use functionality, fluid and multiple circulation systems, and the opportunity to commandeer new spatial relationships within the skyscraper archetype.

Studio Daniel Libeskind finally won the master site plan competition, his multiple towers surrounding the empty footprints of the two lost towers and initially expressing the historic slurry basement wall bounding the depressed memorial park. Fig. 2.37 – Fig. 2.38 Notwithstanding the visual drama of trapezoidal plans, diagonally inscribed skins, sloped tops and torqued vertical shafts, as in the case of his Freedom Tower, the skyscrapers were nevertheless disparate point towers set upon the ground. Libeskind's proposal exhibited fluid open space at street level with a series of mid-height pavilions incorporating a cultural facility, transportation hub and various retail services.

Among the many schemes ultimately presented in the competition, exhibitions and media events that followed were innovative proposals to expand the programmatic and spatial possibilities of the vertically organized building type. United Architects, an ad hoc consortium of progressive firms from Amsterdam, London, Los Angeles and New York, proposed a collection of tilting spires constructed of square plans melding into each other at various points high above street level. The square plans all contained a common module for both elevator cores as well as commercial office space. The towers were connected at the ground plane, at the fourteenth level, and at the amenities-rich "sky park" on the fifty-seventh level. As square floor plans became fused with others, larger floor configurations were created to accommodate differing occupancies with various size requirements.

The tangency of each of the towers created additional lateral structural stability and was intended to improve safety by maximizing access routes from any point within the buildings to a number of exits. The buildings combined twenty-foot-wide central structural cores wrapped at the perimeter in an exoskeletal frame, which created a "tube within a tube" support system. The overall scheme achieved great variety at the exterior and within its interior volume, multiplied horizontal interconnectivity, yet was based upon a simple and repetitive square plan module. The proposal was among the most conceptually elegant: new effects with standard parts.

A similar scheme by SOM, Sejima and Nishizawa and others proposed a dense ensemble of nine towers comprised of trapezoidal plans that became square plans, torqued and bent as they ascended. The towers, imaginatively sited, created interconnecting bridges at multiple locations and suggested multi-story volumes within. Each of the roofs of the towers was fully landscaped, totaling sixteen acres of gardens above the street. Fig. 2.39

Perhaps the most abstract and iconic scheme of all came from the team of Richard Meier, Peter Eisenman, Charles Gwathmey and Steven Holl. Highly geometric, the concept consisted of five identical towers connected by multi-floor sky bridges at regular vertical intervals. Two of the towers were connected and co-planar, as were the other three. Each ensemble was placed at ninety degrees to the other. In many ways, this scheme was the most elementary of all those presented. Fig. 2.41 It left a significant amount of the ground plane undisturbed, extruded the simple rectangularity that is much of lower Manhattan and the commercial office high-rise type, created large floors for trading and business conferencing, and provided a clear strategy for its own structural support. While the apparent and simple geometry of the scheme clearly reflected the work of both Meier and Gwathmey, the grid has frequently been the reference point for the multiple variations in Eisenman's work, as well. Projects such as Holl's interconnected Parallax Towers project of 1990, as well as his 2000 extension to the Sarphatistraat Office Building in Amsterdam, seem familiar to this project. Finally, the fact that this team of strongly opinionated practitioners came together to propose a single archetypal proposal, is reminiscent of the collaborative efforts of Rockefeller Center's Associated Architects, seventy years earlier.

With characteristic sleight of hand, the Ground Zero scheme proposed by Rem Koolhaas and OMA adapted the wedding cake profile of the 1931 Downtown Athletic Club, described in Koolhaas' *Delirious New York* as a rich example of vertical mixed-used programming in a tall building, and turned it on its head. Fig. 2.40 Three upside-down towers create heretofore unimagined possibilities. The ground plane is opened up while the narrow bases of the three columnar buildings plant themselves lightly in the generous plaza at street level. As the floor plates expand skyward, they begin to intersect, expanding floor configurations and multiplying cross circulation. Ironically, these also become the most profitable skyscraper machines imaginable: narrow at the base where the rents are lower, and wider and bigger at the top where rents are at their maximum. They all crown at one continuous roof deck, landscaped and accessible in the best tradition of Le Corbusier.

Notes

[1] Goldberger, Paul, *The Skyscraper,* (King's Dream of New York, Harry Pettit, from King's Views of New York, 1908-09.), op. cit., 2.

[2] Etlin, Richard A., *Modernism in Italian Architecture,* 1890-1940, op. cit., 88.

[3] Goldberger, Paul, *The Skyscraper,* (A drawing of Starrett's proposed 100-story building as it appeared in the New York Herald, May 13, 1906.), op. cit., 10.

[4] Larson, Erik, *The Devil in the White City,* op. cit., 221.

[5] Sadler, Simon, *Archigram: Architecture without Architecture,* op. cit., 4.

[6] Lynn, Greg, *The Talented Mr. Tracer, Tracing Eisenman* (ed. Cynthia Davidson), op. cit. 222.

Fig. 2.1 "King's Dream of New York", from King's Views of New York, 1909, Harry M. Pettit.

Fig. 2.2 The Future Circulation and the Skyscrapers of New York, August 31, 1913.

Fig. 2.3 View of the City, from "Metropolis", 1927.
Fritz Lang, director, Erich Kettelhut, set designer.

Au profil d'une maison telle que le mode de construction en gradins permettrait d'en édifier dans une rue de 8 mètres, on a superposé, en ligne de traits (▪▪▪▪▪▪▪▪), le profil d'une maison ordinaire dans une rue de même largeur. Le grisé foncé correspond à la maison actuelle de la rue Vavin.

Au moyen âge.   Aujourd'hui.   Demain ?

TROIS ÉPOQUES, TROIS TYPES DE MAISONS ET DE RUES

ce gabarit, donner neuf étages à la maison de la rue Vavin. Mais nos fonctionnaires ont décidé que, pour avoir le droit de bâtir en gradins ou en décrochement au-dessus de 15 mètres, il est nécessaire de bâtir verticalement jusque-là. Ce qui revient à défendre de donner de l'air et de la lumière au septième ou huitième étage sans en priver les étages inférieurs.

Quoique n'ayant pas été réalisée dans sa conception intégrale, la maison à gradins revient à un prix qui a permis une réduction de 25 à 30 % sur le taux normal des loyers. Ce résultat est dû en partie à des procédés de construction ou d'aménagement tout à fait nouveaux.

Après avoir établi les murs extérieurs, on a divisé le terrain, par des perpendiculaires à la rue, en intervalles sensiblement égaux de 8 à 10 mètres de largeur. Sur chacune de ces lignes on a élevé des poutres inclinées en béton armé, formant comme le limon de l'escalier, où viennent s'appuyer des piliers qui supportent les poutres parallèles à la rue et le plancher. Les piliers portant un étage traversent,

sans y être liés, les étages inférieurs : chaque étage se trouve ainsi porté séparément, et aucun d'eux ne reçoit la charge des étages supérieurs. On a pu dès lors réduire les murs intérieurs dans une grande proportion et sans inconvénient pour les locataires. Car, en posant les parquets sur du béton, en employant aussi du béton pour les cloisons séparant deux appartements voisins, on a rendu la maison complètement insonore.

D'autre part, on a mis des radiateurs dans toutes les pièces, et on a supprimé les cheminées. Économie : 80.000 francs.

On a supprimé de même les sculptures, les corniches en « pâtisserie », les faux lambris, en un mot tout le faux luxe qui revient fort cher. Les appartements, de lignes très sobres, sont remis aux locataires les murs nus, enduits avec beaucoup de soin, coupés simplement par un stylobate, une moulure et une baguette à hauteur de corniche. Chacun fait sa décoration comme il l'entend.

Enfin, MM. Sauvage et Sarazin ont complété

leur programme par une innovation empruntée à la forme coopérative.

On admet en général que les non-valeurs provenant des appartements vides atteignent à peu près 20 % du revenu brut. On peut donc abaisser le loyer si l'on est sûr que les appartements sont toujours loués. Pour arriver à ce résultat, les architectes ont imaginé de former une société entre plusieurs personnes désireuses d'habiter un même immeuble. Le locataire est en même temps actionnaire, par conséquent copropriétaire ; il a droit à une réduction proportionnelle sur le tarif des loyers. Celui qui aura, par exemple, souscrit 50.000 francs aura droit à une réduction de 2.500 francs. Il sera donc logé pour rien si tel est le prix de son appartement, et il touchera en outre un dividende.

Est-il bien nécessaire d'ajouter que, dans ce nouvel immeuble, dont le plan général est breveté, et qu'il est difficile de juger avant de l'avoir habité, il n'y a déjà plus un appartement à louer !

F. HONORÉ.

Les terrasses, telles qu'elles sont actuellement et telles qu'elles pourront être aux beaux jours prochains.

LA MAISON AUX JARDINS SUSPENDUS

Fig. 2.4 Terraced apartment buildings, Rue Vavin, from "L'Illustration", Paris, March 20, 1914. Henri Sauvage and Charles Sarazin.

Fig. 2.5 Group of Low-Cost Housing projects for the City of
Paris at 13 Rue des Animaux, Paris, 1922. Henri Sauvage.

Fig. 2.6 Terraced apartment buildings proposal, March 30, 1914.
Antonio Sant'Elia.

LUNA PARK AT NIGHT, CONEY ISLAND, N.Y.

RESTAURANT GARDENS

Fig. 2.7 Luna Park skyline by night, Coney Island, 1903.
Frederic Thompson and Elmer Dundy.

Fig. 2.8 A drawing of Starrett's proposed 100-story
building as it appeared in the "New York Herald",
May 13, 1906. Theodore Starrett.

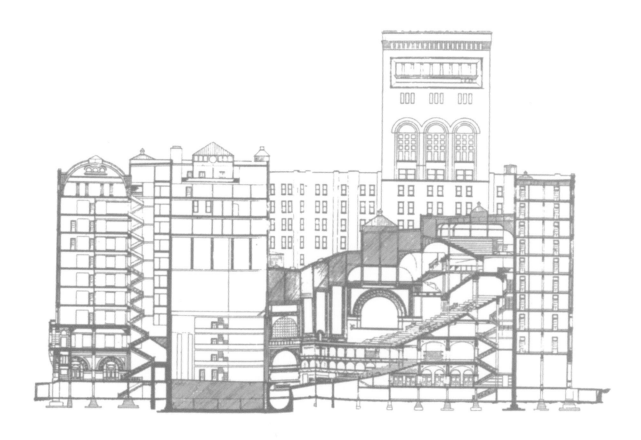

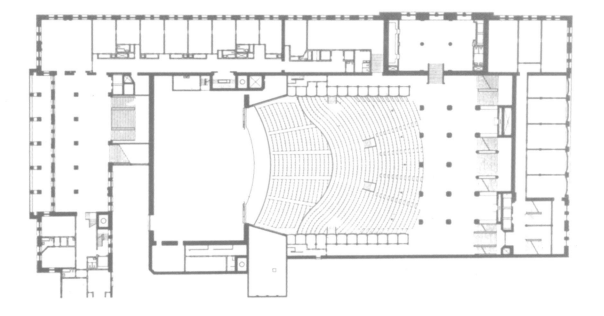

Fig. 2.9 Auditorium Building, longitudinal section and second floor plan, Chicago, 1889. Adler and Sullivan.

Fig. 2.10 Waldorf Astoria Hotel, New York City, 1924.
Schultze and Weaver.

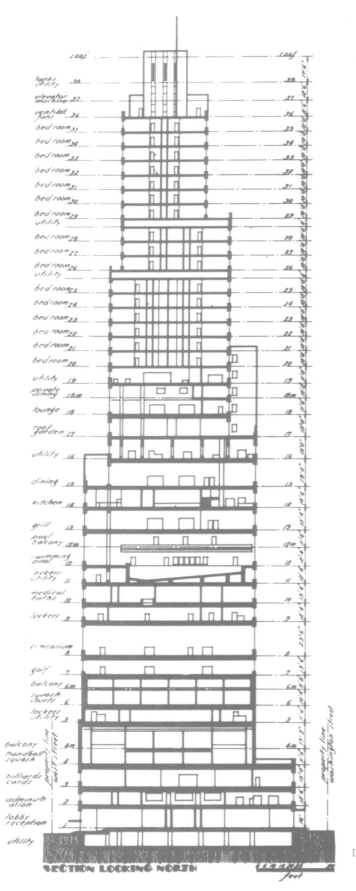

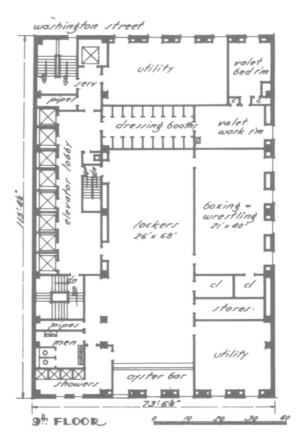

Downtown Athletic Club, plan of ninth floor:

Downtown Athletic Club, section.

Fig. 2.11 **Downtown Athletic Club, New York City, 1931.**
Starrett and Van Vleck, Duncan Hunter.

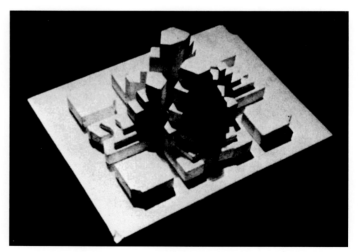

Fig. 2.12 Metropolitan Square proposal, New York City, 1928.
Benjamin Wistar Morris. Fig. 2.13 "The Fling" – Rockefeller
Center, New York City. Raymond Hood.

Fig. 2.14 Rockefeller Center – Scheme 0, New York City,
December 19, 1929. Walter Kilham, Jr.

Fig. 2.15 Birdseye view from 47th Street looking northeast over roof gardens and RCA Building complete with bridges over city streets. John Weinrich, artist.

Fig. 2.16 Rockefeller Center, New York City, 1940.
Reinhard & Hofmeister, Corbett, Harrison & McMurray,
Hood and Godley & Fouilhoux.

Fig. 2.17 Skyscraper proposal for Cap de la Marine, Algiers, 1938.
Le Corbusier.

Fig. 2.18 Unité d'Habitation, elevation. Le Corbusier.

Unité d'habitation, Marseilles

1. Typical cross-section through two inter-
   locking apartments and access corridor
2. Typical plans of two apartments, on three
   levels, indicating how they interlock around
   the access corridor: 1, corridor; 2, entrance;
   3, living room and kitchen; 4, main bedroom
   and bathroom; 5, storage, boiler, drying
   cupboard, ironing and children's shower;
   6, children's bedrooms; 7, void to living
   room below

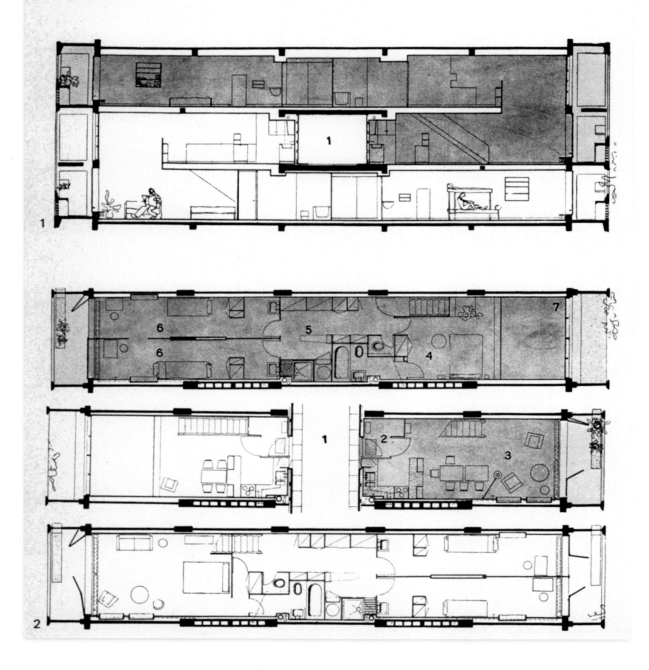

Fig. 2.19 Unité d'Habitation, plans and cross-section,
Marseilles, 1952. Le Corbusier.

Fig. 2.20 Unité d'Habitation, roof terrace. Le Corbusier.
Fig. 2.21 Unité d'Habitation, double-height room and balcony.
Le Corbusier.

Fig. 2.22 Didactic section including the "eye that sees", from "La Ville Radieuse", 1953. Le Corbusier.

Fig. 2.23 Johnson Wax Tower, Racine, Wisconsin 1950.
Frank Lloyd Wright.

Fig. 2.24 Price Tower, Bartlesville, Oklahoma, 1956.
Frank Lloyd Wright.

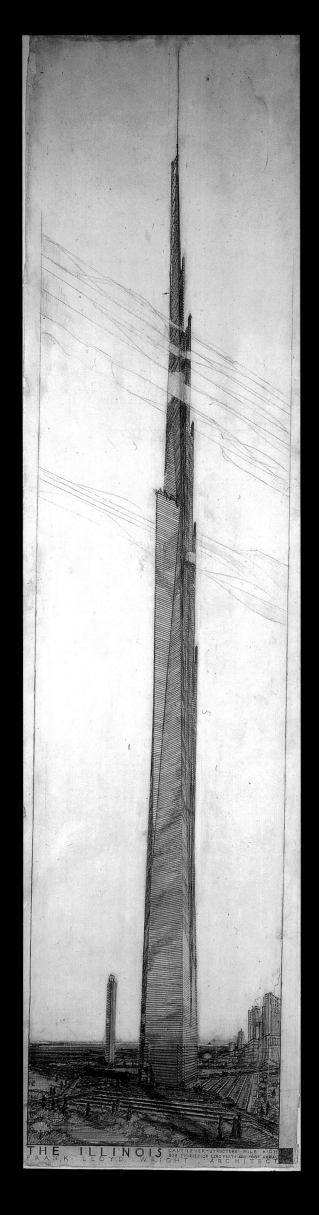

Fig. 2.25 One-Mile-High Skyscraper, 1956. Frank Lloyd Wright.

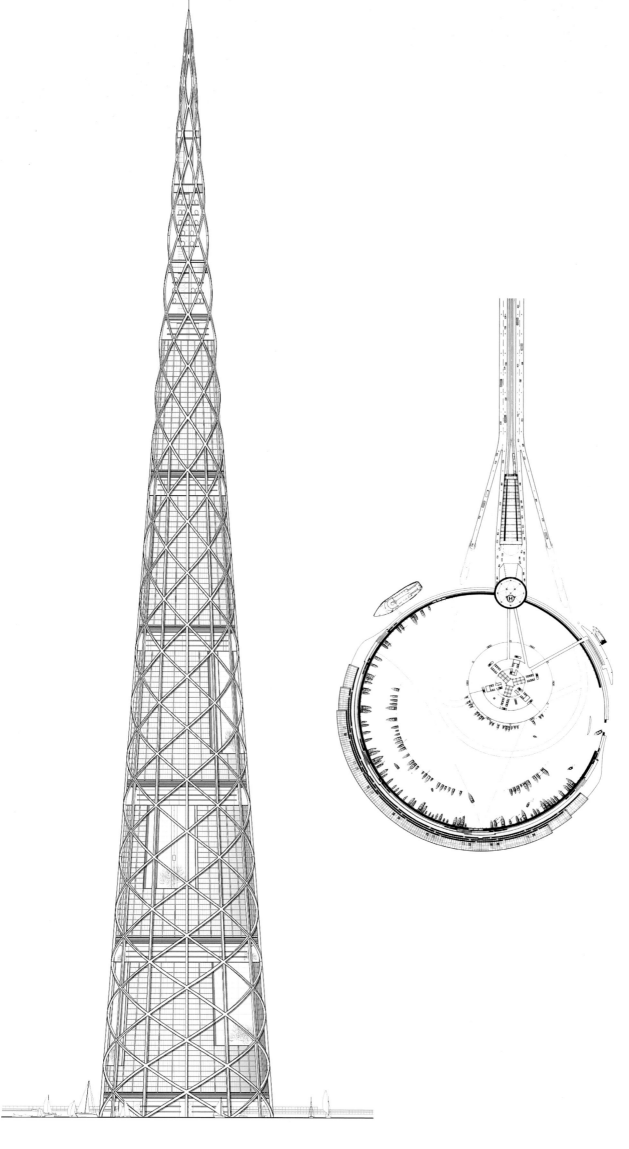

Fig. 2.26 Millennium Tower proposal, Tokyo, 1989.
Foster + Partners.

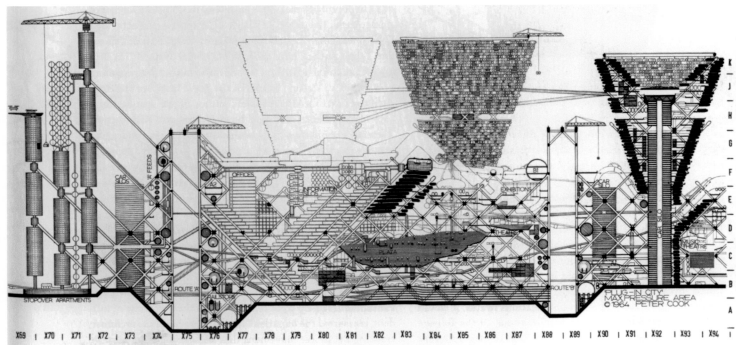

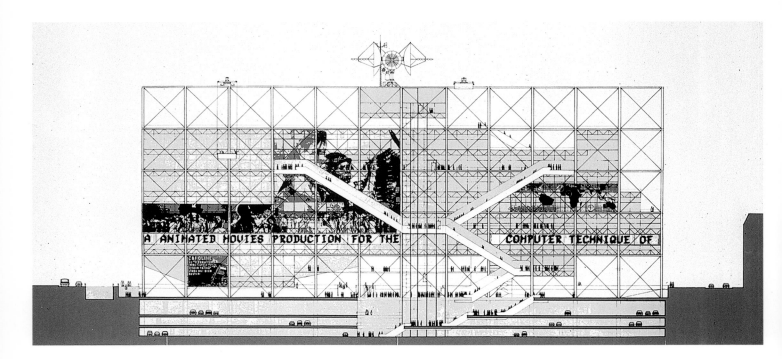

Fig. 2.27 Cities Moving, New York City, 1964. Ron Herron/
Archigram. Fig. 2.28 Plug-In City: Maximum Pressure Area,
1964. Peter Cook/Archigram. Fig. 2.29 Elevation from
the Pompidou Centre competition entry illustrating the concept
of the building as an information centre for Paris and beyond,
Paris, 1977. Piano and Rogers.

Fig. 2.30 **Energy Void**, 1971. Isamu Noguchi.

Fig. 2.31 Max Reinhardt Haus, Berlin, 1992. Peter Eisenman.

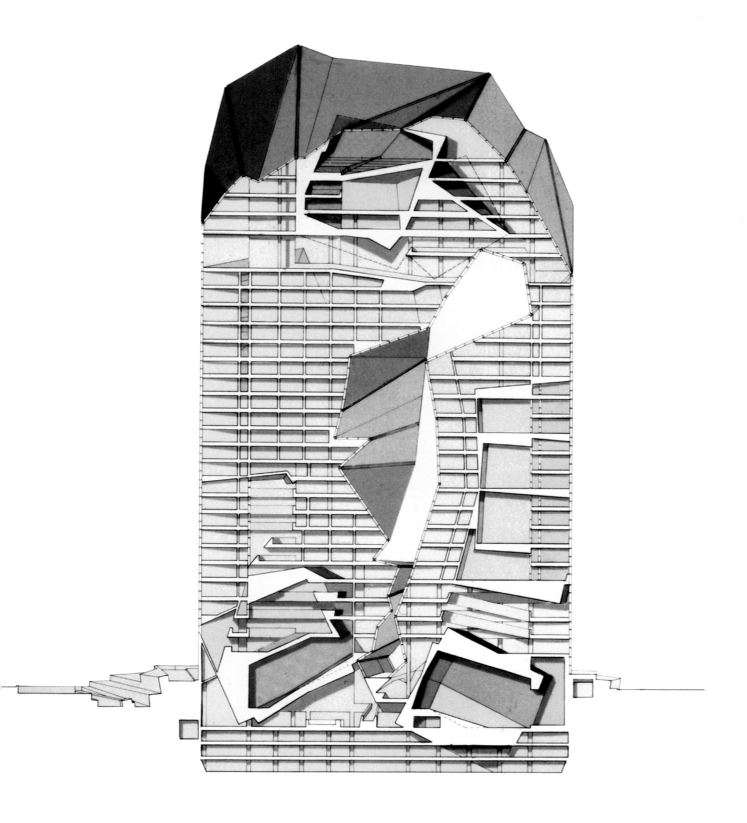

Fig. 2.32 Max Reinhardt Haus. Peter Eisenman.

96

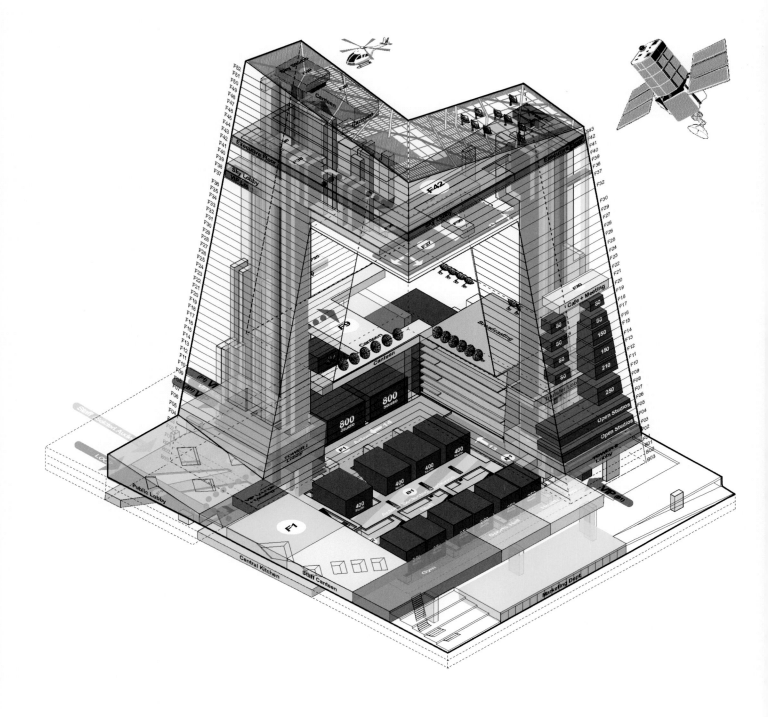

Fig. 2.33 Central Chinese Television Headquarters (CCTV),
Beijing, 2008. Axonometric view of the building. Rem Koolhaas/
Office for Metropolitan Architecture.

Fig. 2.34 CCTV. Rem Koolhaas/Office for Metropolitan Architecture.

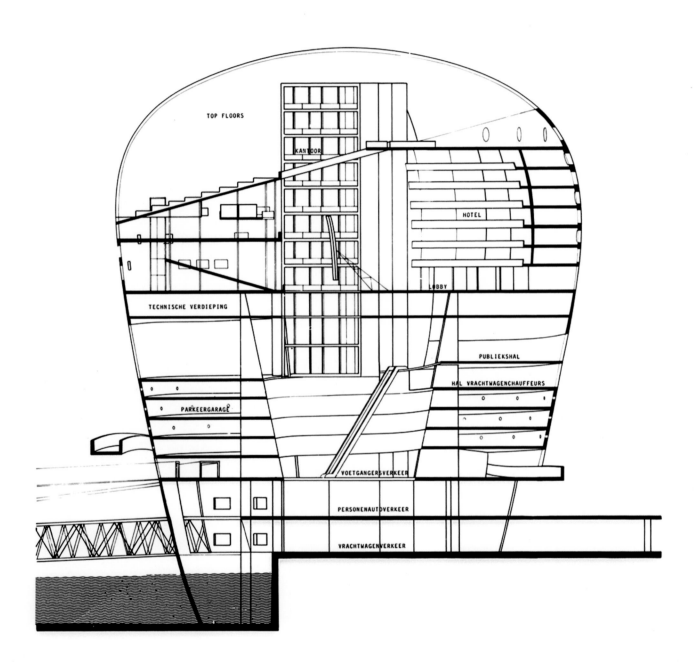

Fig. 2.35 Sea Trade Center, Zeebrugge, Netherllands, 1989.
Rem Koolhaas/Office for Metropolitan Architecture.

Fig. 2.36 Dutch Pavilion, Expo 2000, Hanover, 2000. MVRDV.

Fig. 2.37 World Trade Center, Initial Master Plan Model,
December 18, 2002. Studio Daniel Libeskind.

Fig. 2.38 World Trade Center, interior view of transportation hub, Winning Master Site Plan, Spring 2003. Studio Daniel Libeskind.

Fig. 2.39 World Trade Center, Master Site Plan proposal,
Gardens on the tops of the towers, December 18, 2002.
Skidmore, Owings & Merrill et. al.

Fig. 2.40 World Trade Center proposal, 2002.
Rem Koolhaas/Office for Metropolitan Architecture.

Fig. 2.41 World Trade Center proposal, 2002. Richard Meier & Partners, Eisenman Architects, Gwathmey Siegel & Associates and Steven Holl Architects.

The Environmental Skyscraper

The Enrichment of Vertical Space

Inevitable Skyscraper

We now know that the disruption of regional ecosystems far away can affect our natural systems at home. Global trade has further bound us together, wherein a demand in one part of the world can alter the balance of natural resources in another. From a scientific point of view, sustainability and energy management are now seen as worldwide issues. Nevertheless, human cultures remain distinct and their approaches to these burgeoning issues vary. Great Britain's Norman Foster and Malaysia's Ken Yeang each have a long history of addressing environmental issues in their architecture and yet their strategies and the resulting works are exceedingly different. Exploring these differences highlights cultural attitudes of community, the manmade and the natural, and the role of technology in sustainable living.

Broadly speaking, the industrial application of fossil fuels in the nineteenth century set the developing world on a path of seeing nature as a resource for consumption rather than conservation and restoration. Rapidly urbanizing cities established parks and limited natural systems within their borders as symbols of nature while broadly exploiting nature elsewhere as a source of energy.

Water, wind and gravity historically provided energy sources. In the industrial age, drilling and mining interests continued to identify non-renewable sources that appeared inexhaustible. In the building arena, technological developments such as the emergence of glass and window wall systems, artificial lighting, and heating ventilating and cooling equipment, combined to so significantly alter the potentially negative effects of weather, that fuel-intensive systems were deemed ideal. At the time, they were inexpensive and considered infinitely renewable. As a result, buildings could be much larger, which is to say deeper in plan, as adequate task light no longer depended upon proximity to windows. Building orientation was now considered unimportant as various solar effects could be neutralized by inexpensive mechanical systems. Buildings grew larger and more energy-intensive in their construction and operation as they now became more or less hermetic to the natural world outside. By the middle of the twentieth century, a critical literature began to emerge around the idea that unfettered industrialization and commercialization, monolithic capitalism, and the exploitation of natural systems was unsustainable. Works by Ian McHarg, E.F. Schumacher and Jane Jacobs, as well as a reissue of D'Arcy Thompson's early twentieth century writings, began to attract wider popular attention. Rachel Carson's 1962 *Silent Spring* charged that "'the control of nature' (was) a phrase conceived in arrogance, born of the Neanderthal age of biology and the convenience of Man."

In 1973, the Arab Oil Embargo doubled the cost of crude oil worldwide and created an energy crisis throughout the West. In the 1980s, climatologists began to discover and measure the effects of carbon emissions on the destruction of the earth's protective ozone layer. During that time, the meltdown at Chernobyl's nuclear plant occurred and the Exxon Valdez ran aground in the pristine waters of Prince William Sound, spilling 11 million gallons of crude oil. In the 1990s, the United States Green Building Council (USGBC) was formed and initiated a series of demonstration projects, and the Kyoto Protocol was signed by most nations in the world. In 1999, the USGBC created the pilot Leadership in Energy and Environmental Design program (LEED). In 2002, the Packard Foundation Report recommended that any building owner who held improved property for more than twenty years would benefit financially by designing and building at a LEED Platinum level, irrespective of health and productivity benefits. Today there is much informed literature regarding the effects of climate change and the enormous costs to life and property. It is a matter of grave international concern that, while industrialized nations use the vast majority

of non-renewable energy sources, developing nations too are expending increased quantities of cheap energy with little environmental regulation or remediation. The harsh climatic and agricultural side effects of this pollution nevertheless continue to fall disproportionately on the disadvantaged populations of the world.

Recent data from the Department of Energy (DOE) attributes forty percent of energy used in the United States to the building sector, including energy used for electricity generation. Additionally, the use of energy by the building sector is increasing at a rate faster than that of other sectors, such as agriculture, industry and transportation.[1] The taller the building, the DOE reports, the more energy it consumes per square foot. Average energy consumption is approximately fifty percent higher for buildings in the ten-story and higher category than for buildings that are three or fewer floors.

The average urban dweller, however, uses less energy at home than does the average suburban or rural dweller. Transportation use generally drops as building density rises, and, more importantly, high-rise buildings contain more than twice the number of occupants per square foot on average than low-rise buildings. Increasing the number of occupants per square foot in an office setting improves efficiency on one level but proportionately increases the amount of computer and office equipment, adding to the total energy load. The answer as to how to clearly optimize, or minimize, energy usage in a tall building is not yet an easy one to calculate.

Lighting is responsible for half the electricity used in commercial buildings. The ability to maximize the utility of natural light, to use energy-efficient sources and task-based systems, and to zone lighting grids and reduce their operations by means of sensors have an effect on the ultimate energy expense. However, these savings come at the end of a long series of conversions and manufacturing processes. Issues, such as evaluating the relative efficiency of distributed systems of energy generation for a building over the efficiency of a centralized system, plus the prospect of a state-of-the-art power plant, can drive much greater overall savings than end-of-the-line product selection or energy management. In short, the green skyscraper may be an oxymoron. The role of the architect is not only to find every opportunity to reduce the total energy consumed by the operation of the skyscraper but to minimize the embodied energy of its construction. As long as small energy-saving choices, however, are represented as heroic efforts by the marketing programs which sell commercial space in tall buildings, larger opportunities for energy conservation will be overlooked and less research will be done on the topic.

Central to a tall building's environmental interface is its skin. The understanding of a building's skin as a discrete system began as early as the mid-nineteenth century, prior to any development in curtain wall systems. Gottfried Semper, in his seminal work of 1860, *Style, in the Technical and Tectonic Arts; or, Practical Aesthetics*, formulated a division in the conception of architecture between load-bearing structure and cladding, reflecting on the historic lineage of nomadic tents, animal pens and Laugier's primitive hut of timbers clad with woven roof and wall. We know that the glass skin construction of industrial, garden and exhibition pavilions began at about the time of Semper's writings, and were built less for environmental performance than for expediency, sunlight and visual effects. By the latter half of the nineteenth century, these industrialized techniques began to influence the design of elements within more conventional buildings, namely skylights and atria walls. At the same time, the separation of steel frame and curtain wall was overtaking the historic masonry bearing wall in pursuit of lesser weight and greater building height.

This development constituted a watershed of change. Tall buildings could now achieve much greater heights with little material effect on the structural implications of the lower floors. Steel column and frame sizes grew slightly, but exterior walls at each plan level remained the same depth because they were now anchored to the frame rather than bearing the cumulative gravity forces of everything above them. The skyscraper could now be thought of, not only figuratively but literally, as an extrusion of identical floors, a conception that had both an economic and architectural corollary. As these new realities were absorbed by architects and builders, a more intimate relationship between commerce and architecture followed. Window sizes could now be widened, opening up the interior of the building at all floors to greater views and larger quantities of natural light. Building depths could increase as more natural light could penetrate further into the tower.

The architectural possibilities of a building's exterior immediately changed as the historic pattern of solid masonry walls punctuated by a grid of small windows was overturned by tall building elevations expressing more glass than opaque wall. As long-span high-strength steel frames became the norm, a building's perimeter could be easily cantilevered beyond the edge of the outer columns, allowing a building exterior to be richly articulated at will. While ultimately this new-found freedom led to several generations of flat flush buildings in pursuit of better economics and a new architecture, initially,

this area of invention allowed for the development of the Chicago bay window epitomized by the Reliance Building, as well as the sculpted shafts of New York skyscrapers, such as the Singer and Woolworth buildings.

The most radical and complete vision made possible by these technical developments was put forward in the 1920s by European rationalists Le Corbusier, Mies van der Rohe and Ludwig Hilberseimer. They imagined all-glass towers inserted into the medieval European city. Expressionist architects, such as Hermann Finsterlin, Paul Scheerbart and Bruno Taut discovered a kind of visual alchemy within the all-glass building, which could be luminous, crystalline and overlaid with color. Not long thereafter, architects more fully engaged in industrial design practices such as Jean Prouve and Buckminster Fuller continued to pursue the idea of the lightweight all-glass building. In all cases, these images of the skyscraper upended the traditional neoclassical discourses of composition and appealed to the emerging spirit of democracy and material positivism. Tall, pure, transparent and new, these icons epitomized a new ethos.

The thermal and energy performance of all-glass buildings was, if ignored at the time, a negative consequence. Joined to other developments, such as the proliferation of air conditioning, artificial lighting systems and a kind of Taylorist flexibility associated with the modern office interior, the new glass paradigm for tall buildings appeared capable of fully divorcing itself from the natural environment except for its consumption of increasing quantities of energy. Seemingly self-sufficient and universally applicable, the commercial glass skyscraper could be located anywhere, sited at will and oriented in any direction, and planned to accommodate any range of tenants of any size.

These qualities merged to create an identifiable and physical program for both commercial real estate and architecture. Technical developments, such as structural self-supporting glass, load-bearing silicon sealant, neoprene, and various glass coatings, tints and tempering techniques emerged, altering, among other things, the migration of heat and light into the building interior. In the past twenty years, and with a growing interest in more substantial and refined approaches to energy efficiency, curtain wall developments have gone on to include thermal and encapsulated window-wall systems, embedded light and heat blind technologies, the return of operable systems for natural ventilation, and spectrally specific glass coatings that maximize natural light, filter out selective wavelengths and repel incident heat. The exterior skin of a contemporary building is increasingly capable of being designed and installed to address the many tasks assigned to it. Chief among these are lighting, ventilation, protection from humidity, insulation against heat and cold, wind, sun and glare protection, visual privacy, transparency, prevention of mechanical damage, sound protection, fire protection, and energy management.[2]

Notwithstanding the demonstrative claims of new building sponsors that significant gains in the efficient use of energy are being made in their tall buildings, the ability to accurately measure a skyscraper's total impact on energy usage, or its net contribution to the depletion of fossil fuels, remains unclear. Important questions are unanswered. Irrespective of the amount of energy required to operate it, can a tall building even be considered green, given the enormous embodied energy expended in its production? Can the collateral benefits of its dense urban location, such as the availability of public transportation, the presence of mixed-use services, shared infrastructures, and the longevity of historic structures, outweigh the expense its embodied energy? And, if not, what other models of efficient habitation might we compare it to? Finally, how valid is the proposition of a Zero-Energy Building (ZEB) such as SOM's Pearl River Tower in Guangzhou, China, a concept that the energy consumption within a building is presumably zero if the building is capable of generating enough energy within its boundaries to fulfill its own uses. Many of these projects' sponsors go so far as to advertise that they have the ability to put excess power back into the regional utility grid. These claims generally stem from monetary calculations alone and fail to measure the possibly higher energy costs embodied in the same advanced technical systems that aim at lowering the operating energy budget. Tall buildings, even as symbols of American-style optimism and public relations, cannot yet be considered net producers of energy.

Despite the enormous media coverage given to green issues and the general popularity of the topic, the federal government has yet to establish any standards by which to regulate energy efficiency. Various state, county and city agencies have stepped in to create their own regulations, as have university systems, public and private institutions, and corporations. Over the past seven years, some forty states have adopted new building codes, dedicated to the reduction of energy consumption in major buildings. LEED certification is required for all new buildings constructed by the General Services Administration (GSA), and the cities of Boston, Washington D.C., San Francisco and Los Angeles have recently required all new buildings over 50,000

square feet to be LEED certified and many other cities are following suit. Generally, and perhaps predictably, America has been unregulated in this area. Where regulations or standards have been established, these actions are generally in response to a perceived desire on the part of consumers for higher standards in the commercial marketplace. As in the case of New York's Hearst Tower, the LEED Gold certificate is a central feature in the sales and public relations literature aimed at differentiating and elevating the building's position in a competitive and upscale market. Many new high-rise residences are beginning to display either environmentally friendly features or LEED certification. As buyers purchase real estate in much the same manner as consumers secure retail brands, many identify with a label of environmental responsibility and the liberal ethos of which it is a part. Developers supported by a team of behavioral strategists and marketing professionals fully grasp these positive associations and construct broad, compelling narratives directed toward prospective sales.

Mark Wigley, Dean of Columbia's Graduate School of Architecture, goes so far as to predict that if change occurs in America, it won't be driven by politicians or architects but by the real estate developers.[3] In fact, it is possible now to imagine a time when developers are compelled to achieve LEED certification for fear of failing to translate their projects into signifiers of "the best and the brightest" within the marketplace. Also, as various state energy codes have been periodically revised and made more stringent, it appears certain that LEED standards will be revised upward in the future and additional programs will be added that will provide more exclusive levels of differentiation for the more discriminating buyers. In New York City alone, an array of elite projects from the Durst Organization's Condé Nast Building, Renzo Piano's New York Times Headquarters, the Bank of America Tower at One Bryant Park, Cesar Pelli's Solaire, and Robert Stern's Tribeca Green all employ wide-ranging features to convey their putative environmental leadership.

It is worth saying that within the American tall building model, these prevalent approaches to energy awareness, while not insignificant, are conveyed to us as part of the broader retail medium. The principal environmental narrative of these projects in general, and the LEED rating system in particular, form predictable lists of features that, in effect, "one can choose to buy," bringing higher ratings and, within a certain audience, higher prestige. Not surprisingly, a widening array of ever more advanced technologies and products for purchase are

continually being made available. The eminent-
ly sellable turn-of-phrase, "high-performance
building" has entered the development lexicon,
implying that the greatest good flowing from
a building's environmental sensitivity is its
technologically advanced character or image
for which the most discriminating and capable
consumers would traditionally pay more.

As we consider the incremental steps taken
within our market-based culture to mediate
the skyscraper and our current concerns of
environmental degradation, it is informative
to review the contributions of other cultures
which generate their own belief systems and
sense of possibility. Two prominent architects of environmental skyscrapers, Norman
Foster and Ken Yeang, approach their projects
from different perspectives, with Foster
building on Europe's mainstream technological
tradition, and Yeang, a bi-cultural Asian
architect, attempting to interpret the skyscraper in light of biological concepts and
a Southeast Asian perspective.

Norman Foster

Following architectural school at Yale,
and brief stints working on urban renewal
projects in the United States, Norman
Foster returned to his native Britain in 1963
to begin his own practice in architecture.
Initially founded as Team 4, with his wife
Wendy Foster, Richard Rogers and Georgie
Wolton, one of Foster's first projects was
the 1966 Creek Vean House in Feock,
Cornwall. Fig. 3.1 The house, facing south
onto a broad estuary, was partially buried
in the ground, its roofs heavily planted.
Rooms were organized along the spines of
top-lit picture galleries, providing borrowed
light into the adjacent rooms, while large
sliding walls permitted additional light and
access. This early project displayed Foster's
abiding interest in architecture formed
through the interplay of technology, flexibility and environmental sensitivities. Many
of these same lessons were taken up years
later in his 1991 underground Crescent
Wing extension to the Sainsbury Centre
for Visual Arts in Norwich, England.

Having created Foster Associates in 1967,
he was commissioned to design the small
but pivotal Willis Faber & Dumas Office in
Ipswich, Suffolk, in 1973. Fig. 3.2 – Fig. 3.3
While only a three-story structure, the
building represented in many ways the seeds
of skyscrapers to come, all the while recalling the alluring images of earlier skyscrapers
theorized by van der Rohe and Le Corbusier.
Sited at the edge of the medieval street
pattern of Ipswich, the building's perimeter
and exterior window wall take on the streets'
organic and curvilinear form. Foster wrapped
this form in mullionless butt-glazing, removing

all of the conventional aluminum extrusions
into which a glass wall is conventionally set,
and replaced them with interior structural
glass fins and clips. The glass is tinted so that,
while by day it projects a monolithic solidity,
at night the light within radiates out and
dematerializes the skin, exhibiting the glowing
contents of the building to the outside.

A large central skylight pierces the center
of the building through which natural light
falls and travels as reflected light throughout
an interior of open-plan floors. This atrium
becomes the interior social focus for the
office and carries the vertical transportation
system from ground floor to the planted
roof where employees can meet, enjoy the
rooftop restaurant and recreate. On the
ground floor sits a fitness center, swimming
pool and coffee bar.

This three-story extruded office building
synthesizes both the early modernist dream
for skyscrapers as well as the mixed-use
and sustainable model of the present day.
Highly technological and iconic, all-glass,
with a landscaped and usable rooftop, the
"little tower" makes available multiple uses to
its inhabitants, uses natural light to its fullest
within a modern and flexible open-office floor
plan, and, in its programming, it is socially
responsive and sustainable. From today's
perspective it is not difficult to see how
prescient this building was and how it has
been both copied and expanded in buildings
of greater height and density.

In 1971, Foster collaborated with
Buckminster Fuller on the Climatroffice
project, a biospheric envelope in which trays
of office floors were internally supported,
freeing them from the technical and environmentally responsive skin that was planned
to comfort the occupants and manage
the entry of natural light. Fig. 3.4 Again, a
central atrium was introduced, bringing light
into the middle of broad floor plates and
enjoining vertical circulation and social
interface. The ground level, perimeters
of the trays and the top levels all exhibit
plantings which take advantage of incident
natural light. Vague suggestions are made
of a Fuller-inspired triangulated structural
system, later to become Foster's hallmark
exterior "diagrid," with helipad and telecommunications equipment frankly expressed
at the top of the building.

The clearly drawn, if modest, lessons of
Willis Faber & Dumas, plus a growing resume
of technologically inspired buildings, led
to Foster's 1981 commission for the extraordinary Hong Kong and Shanghai Banking
Corporation Headquarters in Hong Kong.
Fig. 3.5 Dubbed at the time the "world's most
expensive building," the legible, if highly
exercised, display of technology, the naturally
lit fifty-two-meter-high central atrium, the

inherent flexibility of the open plan, and the array of multiple uses within the building all brought the lessons of Willis Faber & Dumas into the realm of the contemporary skyscraper. In this tower, additional technologies were employed in an attempt to integrate aspects of the natural environment. Its central air conditioning system, for example, is supplemented with a deep below-grade tunnel which pumps sea water from the bay and uses it as a primary coolant. Fixed aluminum louvers shade the exterior glazing, while a "sun scoop," powered by a computer programmed with solar timetables, reflects light into the building's center using twenty arrays, each having twenty-four mirrors. This device was further developed in Foster's 1999 rehabilitation of The Reichstag in Berlin. The entire tower is raised twelve meters above the ground plane allowing the base of the building to act as shaded open space, providing access and a visual corridor to adjacent properties and rights-of-way.

The eight-story ITN Headquarters in London from 1991, while a more modest mid-rise infill building, continues to exhibit design strategies to manipulate natural light and heat. Fig. 3.6 – Fig. 3.7 A central and terraced atrium provides natural light throughout the workspace while providing a social center for the multi-tenant building. Double-layered insulating glass with unusually deep cavities protects the interior from heat while maximizing sunlight. Adjustable silver blinds provide human interface and control. The ITN building displays Foster's interest in breaking down taller buildings into vertical neighborhoods or in effect, a series of smaller mid-rise neighborhoods. This tendency is nowhere better exhibited than in his 1997 design of Europe's tallest building at the time, the Commerzbank Headquarters in Frankfurt, Germany. Fig. 3.8 - Fig. 3.9

Commerzbank is one of Germany's "big three" private-sector banks. Foster was commissioned in the mid-'90s to design its new headquarters, retaining the nearby former headquarters building from the 1970s, and establishing a heretofore un-achieved level of environmental performance. In accordance with Germany's stringent building regulations which exceed anything seen in the U.S., the bank mandated a natural ventilation supplement to air conditioning systems and a maximum of daylighting and outside visual access for its employees.

Foster's design response resulted in a slightly bowed triangular plan with rounded corners in which vertical circulation, freight, support and convenience facilities were located. Thick lateral shear walls were located in the corners as well, stabilizing the height of this already stable triangular form, and allowing the narrow bands of office space spanning them to be glazed, column-free and maximally illuminated with natural light. Vertical stacks of eight floors of office are distributed radially around the tower and alternate with four-story winter gardens which provide both outward views for office workers as well as interior views to the gardens. These gardens also provide outdoor habitable green decks reminiscent of the early Willis Faber & Dumas rooftop, and oxygenate the tall interior atrium which runs the full height of the building. The decks, spiraling the building and alternating vertically every eight floors, reestablish outdoor social space in mid-rise vertical segments much as the ITN building did in London. Vertical neighborhoods within the larger high-rise community are created.

The central atrium in Commerzbank functions as a vertical flue drawing natural ventilation through the building. Slits in the inner facades draw this ventilation into the air conditioning and heating system. Additional heat recovery pumps keep overall energy consumption to a minimum.

The concept of a vertical ventilation flue has been taken to further ornamental effect in Foster's Swiss Re headquarters at Saint Mary Axe in London. Fig. 3.11 Completed in 2004, the distribution of multiple vertical flues around the exterior of the building, rather than in an interior atrium, grew out of the need to locate the dense elevator and services core within the center of the skyscraper surrounded by a ring of horizontal circulation and office space. Fig. 3.12 The small parcel size typical of the medieval City led to a smaller typical floor plate and caused a compression and reduction in scale of the plan elements, which had been more spacious in Frankfurt's Commerzbank. Initially, Foster proposed that the flues, or atria, be planted and incorporate social spaces, much as he had created in prior buildings. But as the building would ultimately be open to multiple tenants of varying sizes, the decision was made to leave them unplanted with the ability to segregate them from one tenant to the next. Fig. 3.10

The low-energy ventilation system in Swiss Re is further evolved from earlier Foster buildings. The circular and bowed shape of the tower that has become known as the Gherkin allows wind forces to be directed around the building, rather than downward as in typical rectangular towers. This creates a gradation of positive pressures on the windward facade with negative pressures on other sides, setting up a pattern by which natural ventilation can be drawn through the atria and into the office space. Fig. 3.13 Motorized perimeter windows are placed in each atrium and manage the degree of available ventilation and wind speed. This system is backed up by a conventional air conditioning system.

The window glazing is comprised of a low-emissivity double-glazed clear unit on the outside and a single layer of glass on the inside, separated by a cavity between 1.0 and 1.4 meters in depth. Air is extracted from the office space, as well as heat from the metallic-finish Venetian blinds in the cavity, redistributed within the cavity and to the outside by way of an air-handling unit. The air conditioning plant is decentralized per floor, allowing more efficient delivery of comfort at each level and at each solar exposure. The top of the building is completed with a fully glazed dome above a rooftop restaurant, one of Foster's high-rise social spaces with roots back to the earliest modernist visions. Originally, the architect had designed a giant solar shade which was to be installed on the interior of the dome and was engineered to move in response to the sun's rotation but ultimately the glass substrate chosen for the building was tinted and coated in an attempt to reduce heat transmission and the solar shade was not built. The tortile pattern of differently coated glasses was installed as a representation of the swirling atria and has become one of the building's identifiably decorative features.

Finally, Foster and Partners' 2006 Hearst Tower in New York City, if not displaying the architects' most comprehensive thinking with respect to environmental management, shows what is commercially possible within the current marketplace for the archetypal American high-rise office building. Fig. 3.14 – Fig. 3.16 A forty-six-story rectangular extrusion, the building contains typical 20,000-square-foot column-free floor plates with a generally central core, shifted to the west to abut an adjacent building. Fig. 3.14 All floors, except for the intermediate mechanical floor, are functionally interchangeable, and the window wall is a conventionally glazed curtain wall system providing floor-to-ceiling coated insulated glass on a five-foot horizontal planning module. While this office building may work well for the Hearst Corporation, it could serve most any other Class A office tenant looking for space in any urban real estate market. As it is in so many ways a visually striking yet conventional American office tower, it provides us an insight into the realistic possibilities and limitations for addressing sustainability and energy management in the U.S.

One of the various energy management strategies employed by the Hearst Tower design, and largely supported by public agencies and the commercial marketplace from an urban design perspective, is the adaptive re-use of the original historic six-story Hearst Building. The rejuvenation

of the facade and the occupation of ground-level retail supporting the sidewalk, are both an urban recycling strategy as well as an attempt to program the public right-of-way, providing multiple uses as part of a walking experience. The building's secure lobby is raised to the third floor of the existing building with a large sky-lit volume where food and services as well as a second level of secured access to the elevator core is available to the building's occupants.

The lobby is both cooled and heated by way of a radiant system of water-filled pipes beneath the limestone flooring. Additional cooling and humidification are provided by *Icefall,* the lobby water feature designed by artist James Carpenter and Foster Partners, which runs recycled rainwater over a sloped cast-glass wall, releasing water into the indoor air. Rainwater, harvested in a 4,000-gallon reclamation tank in the basement, feeds the fountain, provides evaporative cooling in the office air conditioning system above and irrigates plantings at the exterior.

In pursuit of a LEED Gold certification from the USGBC, many typical measures were employed, in addition to extraordinary ones, to reduce the building's impact on the environment. The majority of the building's structural steel was recycled and the exterior diagrid system reportedly saved 2000 tons of steel overall. The climate control system employs "free air-cooling", using filtered outside air without temperature modification seventy-five percent of the year. Strategic material and technology choices, such as reflective roof pavers, low-E-coated selective spectrum glass and water and electrical sensors contribute to the higher rating. Interior finishes were examined and selected for recycled content, local sourcing and low toxicity. Like many American commercial buildings, a broad menu of strategies and product selections were made to achieve the LEED rating proudly displayed at building entrances and on marketing literature.

Ken Yeang

The career of hard-working Malaysian architect Ken Yeang represents a unique and complex case study with respect to reconciling environmental concerns and the design of the tall building. Yeang was born in Malaysia after World War II and educated from boarding school through the university in the United Kingdom, first at the Architectural Association (AA), and later in a doctoral program at the University of Cambridge. He returned to Malaysia in 1976 to open an architectural practice, T. R. Hamzah & Yeang, with his classmate Tengku Robert Hamzah. He has worked throughout Asia and in England.

Yeang's work in Malaysia and his bi-cultural background highlight numerous issues. In 1957, Malaysia gained independence from Britain, yet Yeang lived and studied for fifteen years in the U.K. Malaysia has since seen both an enormous influx of Western businesses and a series of dramatic economic recessions, most recently in 1997, when the local currency, along with others in Southeast Asia, crashed. This periodic influx and withdrawal of Western investment capital has exacerbated a search for national identity already underway in a post-colonial Malaysia.

Yeang's contacts at the Architectural Association during the 1960s and '70s were studio directors Elia Zenghelis of OMA and Archigram's Peter Cook and Ron Herron. While at the AA, Yeang developed an abiding interest in the works of the Japanese Metabolists, drawn as he was to the prospect of an organic even biological architecture, and one with Asian roots. He spent a brief stint with Ian McHarg at the University of Pennsylvania, much taken with McHarg's iconic 1969 *Design with Nature,* and completed his doctoral dissertation, "A Theoretical Framework for Incorporation of Ecological Considerations in the Design and Planning of the Built Environment." Yeang's characteristic combination of intensity and ambition are well characterized by this title, which was reworked and published in 1995 as *Designing with Nature: The Ecological Basis for Architectural Design.*

Like Norman Foster, Yeang's earliest work was small and local, notably a series of Malaysian homes. Layered and Corbusian in form, they generally incorporated natural ventilation, filtered sunlight and were sited to take advantage of prevailing winds. These early works culminated in his own 1984 home, Roof-Roof House, which displayed many of the features later employed in his tall buildings. Fig. 3.17

Notably, the central form of the Roof-Roof House is a trellised arched roof that spreads over the top of the minor building roofs, unifying the form of the house while providing shade to the many outdoor decks and habitable rooftops below. Deep balcony extensions throw shade on exterior walls, and windows are set into deep frames with large, operable glass windows and doors to accept natural ventilation. With open windows and doors, the extension of balconies and terraces, and the overarching shade trellis, the division of indoor and outdoor space is blurred creating the "environmental filter" Yeang describes in his larger buildings.

From 1984 through 1987, Ken Yeang produced three skyscrapers in Kuala Lumpur, referred to by the architect as his Series One Towers. While undistinguished in many respects, these towers begin to identify the architectural programming he employs in pursuit of a regionally and environmentally responsive skyscraper.

Commissioned in 1981, the twenty-four-story Plaza Atrium is the simplest of the towers. Fig. 3.18 – Fig. 3.19 A white vertical extrusion which grows out of its triangular site, the skyscraper has tinted horizontal window strips characteristic of conventional office towers and an offset elevator core which opens onto an otherwise small floor plate. The unique feature of the building is a series of cavernous and one-sided multi-story atria in the exterior wall of the tower which provide outdoor terraces to be landscaped and occupied, and overhangs that throw the glass walls below into shade. Fig. 3.19 This softening of the edge of the tower wall is what Yeang refers to as the "enclosural valve," or "filter," a permeable zone that allows interaction between interior and exterior elements. At the top of the tallest atrium, the architect has located a characteristic concrete louver, which filters rain and direct sun and permits hot air to disperse.

Another twenty-four-story tower, IBM Plaza, is also unexceptional but for the further development of Yeang's characteristic environmental elements. Fig. 3.20 The architect describes the goals of the building in the following way: "The building does four things. It sets out to respond by plan and form to the climate. It responds to the requirement for landscaping by introducing planting upwards diagonally across the face of a high-rise built form. It seeks to break away from the conventions of a straight plane, curtain walled modernist tower block. In terms of urban design, it relates and provides linkages to the low-rise commercial shophouses surrounding the base and the pedestrian plaza."[4]

The square plan of the tower is sited on a north/south axis. The two vertical cores, which contain elevators, exit stairs, services and convenience facilities, are located outside the square to the east and west sides, where they block the most extreme incident sunlight. In this manner, the cores can also be available to natural ventilation and sunlight while the interior of the plan is open to unencumbered space planning. The ground level of the tower is more richly developed than the Plaza Atrium, with gardens and shaded plazas designed beneath the tower, and the entry is open to natural ventilation. Terraced and planted setbacks occur along the two sides of the building but are little more successful than Yeang's experiment at the Plaza Atrium. A generous roof deck opens up at the top of the building and is covered by one of the architect's characteristic sunshades, struggling to recall the ridged roof of a traditional Malay house.

Menara Boustead, Yeang's thirty-two-story office tower, completed in 1987, adds several more features that further develop the architect's vocabulary. In terms of programming, the building locates banking floors on the bottom two levels for direct retail access, parking facilities, a food court, a fitness center, and a rooftop helipad. Terraces in this building are centrally land-scaped and designed as deep outdoor spaces in the corners created between the radial exterior wall and the orthogonal all-glass wall of the office space. This effect provides deep shade, natural ventilation and the ability to provide maximum glass area onto a highly usable outdoor area. In addition to these perimeter terraces, Yeang experi-ments with periodic multi-story sky-courts at the tower's edge. Once again, the vertical core elements are aligned along the east and west sides of the office plan, becoming thermal buffers to the space within. The exterior cladding on this skyscraper is more advanced: a double-walled aluminum system with a double-ventilated heat sink shield pro-tects the inner wall from heat transmission.

To date, Menara Mesiniaga, a small idiosyn-cratic office tower completed in 1992, and referred to by Yeang as the first of his Series Two Towers, remains for many observers, the most compelling and complete of his built projects. Fig. 3.21 Located on the outskirts of Kuala Lumpur, this fifteen-story office building for a local IBM franchise represents a fuller integration of the various environmental tools with which the architect experimented on earlier towers, while standing apart as an informal and opportunistic vision of architec-ture and high technology. In its image, the student of architecture can sense the wacky optimism of Archigram iconography as well as the obsessive kit-of-parts mentality of Japanese Metabolists. The building's move-ment away from a predisposition toward classic modernist form also renders it newly modern, deconstructed and challenging.

Dubbed by Yeang his first "bioclimatic skyscraper," the circular tower has a tripartite vertical structure. The tilted landscaped base brings the planted ground plane up and into the building over the top of the lobby. In this way, the landscaping of terraces and deep insets above is both more three dimensional and appears to grow out of the ground. The midsection of the tower is comprised of a radial glass curtain wall wrapped with spiral-ing sunshades of varying densities depending on solar exposure and held away from the inner wall to allow for air circulation and deep shade. At the top of the building, deep erosions into the window wall allow for sky courts and accessible shaded terraces, which are crowned by a roof deck and shaded swimming pool. The rooftop tubular steel shade structure is designed to accept an array of photovoltaic panels.

The perimeter structural columns of the Menara Mesiniaga are wrapped in highly finished aluminum panels and held outside the exterior window wall as an exoskeletal system. Windows on the north and south elevations run floor to ceiling, while the elevator core is placed against the easterly elevation of the tower. The tower's highly porous shaft, which Yeang conceives of as a "sieve-like filter," is remotely Corbusian, if only in its evocation of the phrase "a machine for living in."

Two subsequent towers completed in the 1990s, the MBf Tower and the Menara UMNO, both on the island of Penang, were not among Yeang's most complex works. Nevertheless, they further exploit the deep and cavernous spaces that provide both natural ventilation and accessible, plantable outdoor spaces, unite the inside and outdoors, and work to achieve a cohesive image. Fig. 3.22

Whereas most architectural theorists are known to infrequently find actual building commissions with which to explore and test their theories, one suspects that Ken Yeang's career has been quite the reverse. He has perhaps built so much large-scale work within a culture that has allowed him sufficient freedom to improvise the sky-scraper archetype, that his built work of the '80s and '90s has conversely informed his later theoretical presentations and competi-tion entries as he pursues higher levels of theoreti-cal consistency and integration. Among those proposals have been the unbuilt Hitechniaga Headquarters (1995), the eighty-story Tokyo-Nara Tower (1995), the thirty-six-story Shanghai Armoury Tower (1997), the BATC Signature Tower (1998), and master plans for Malaysia's Johor Bahru (1995) and Rostock, Germany's Eco-Tech City (1997).

Fig. 3.24 – Fig. 3.25

Notes

[1] Addington, Michelle, *No Building is an Island*, Harvard Design Magazine Spring/Summer 2007, op. cit., 38.

[2] Lang, Werner, Is it all just a facade? The functional, energetic and structural aspects of the building skin, *In Detail: Building Skins: Concepts, Layers, Materials*, Christian Schittich (Ed.), op. cit., 28.

[3] Ouroussoff, Nicolai, *Why Are They Greener Than We Are?* The New York Times Magazine, May 20, 2007, op. cit., 66.

[3] Yeang, Ken, *Reinventing the Skyscraper: A Vertical Theory of Urban Design*, op. cit., 64.

Fig. 3.1 Creek Vean House, Feock, Cornwall, 1966.
Norman Foster, Wendy Foster, Richard Rogers and
Georgie Wolton (Team Four).

Fig. 3.2 Willis Faber and Dumas Office, Ipswich, 1975.
Foster + Partners.

Fig. 3.3 Willis Faber and Dumas Office. Foster + Partners.

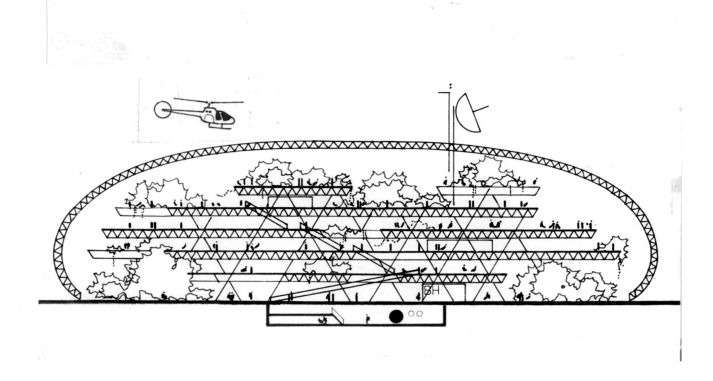

Fig. 3.4 The Climatroffice Project, 1971.
Foster + Partners and Buckminster Fuller.

Fig. 3.5 Hong Kong and Shanghai Banking Corporation
Headquarters, Hong Kong, 1986. Foster + Partners.

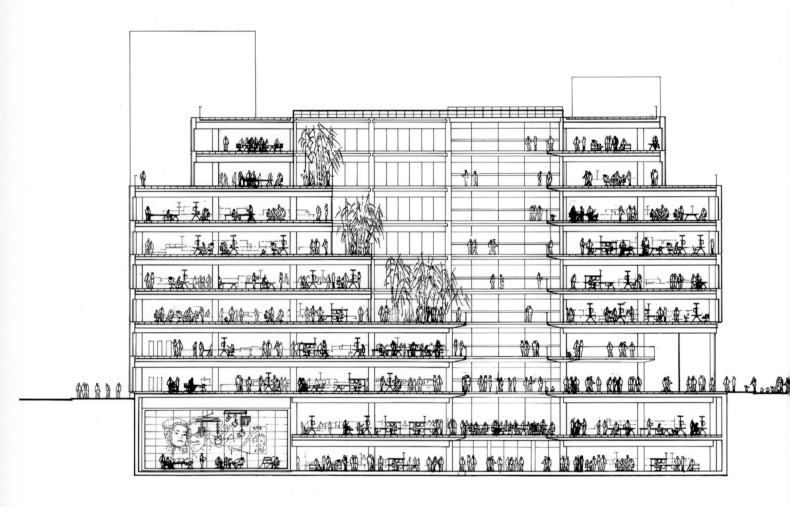

Fig. 3.6 ITN Headquarters, London, 1991. Foster + Partners.

Fig. 3.7 **ITN Headquarters. Foster + Partners.**

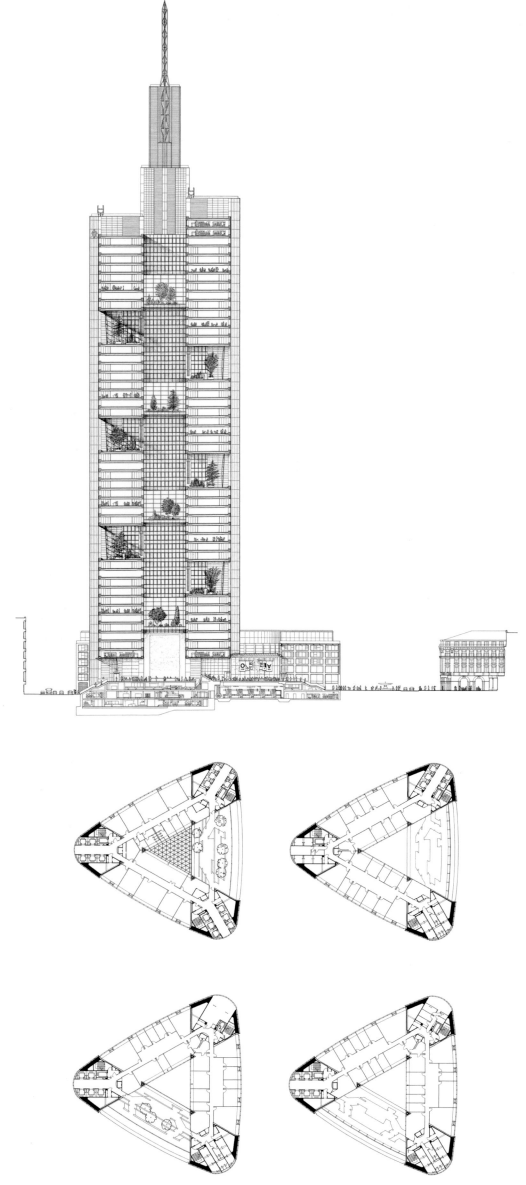

Fig. 3.8 Commerzbank Headquarters,
Frankfurt, 1997. Foster + Partners.

Fig. 3.9 Commerzbank Headquarters, Foster + Partners.

126

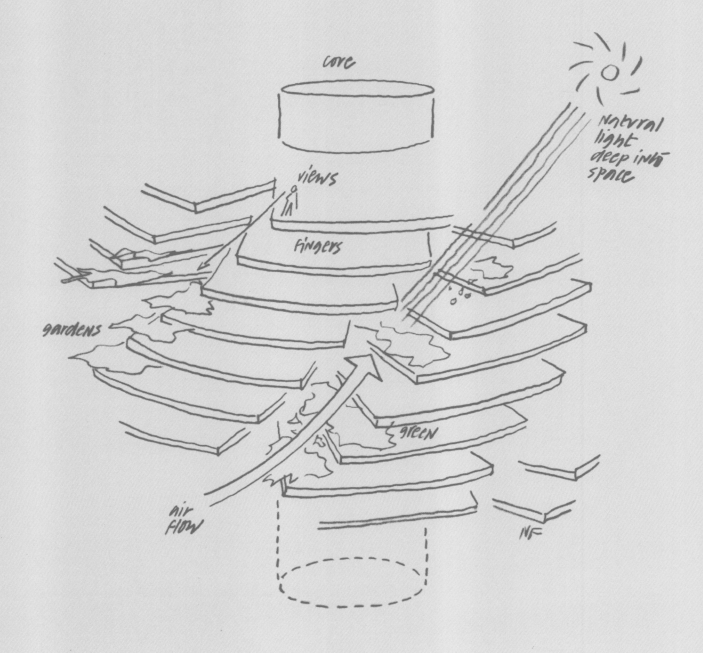

core

views

fingers

natural
light
deep into
space

gardens

green

air
flow

NF

Fig. 3.10 30 St. Mary Axe, concept sketch by
Norman Foster, London, 2004. Foster + Partners.

Fig. 3.11 30 St. Mary Axe, Foster + Partners.

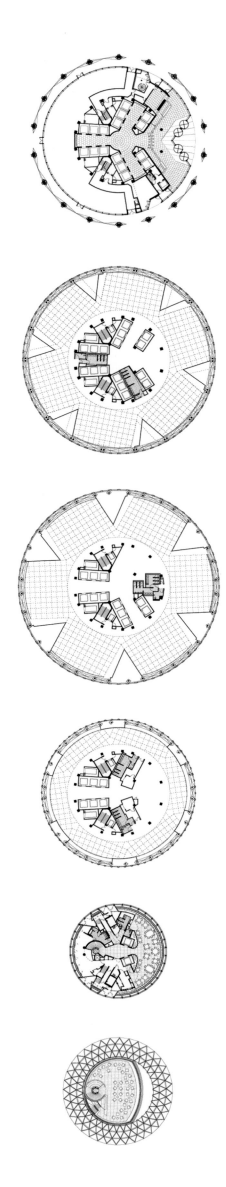

Fig. 3.12 **30 St. Mary Axe, floor plans.** Foster + Partners.

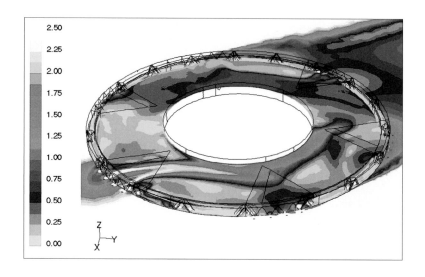

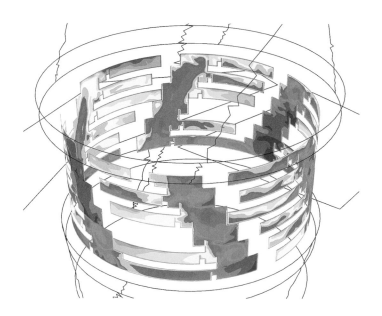

Fig. 3.13 **30 St. Mary Axe, computer models, 2004.**
Foster + Partners.

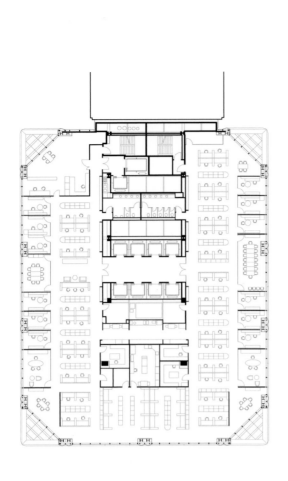

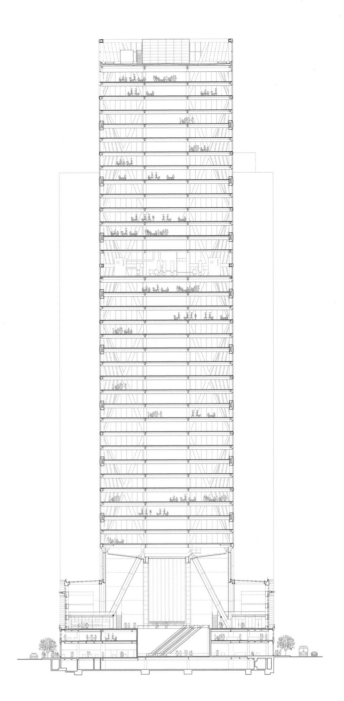

Fig. 3.14 & Fig. 3.15 Hearst Tower. New York City, 2007.
Foster + Partners.

Fig. 3.16 Hearst Tower, Foster + Partners.

Fig. 3.17 Roof-Roof House, Kuala Lumpur, 1984.
Ken Yeang/T. R. Hamzah & Yeang.

Fig. 3.18 Plaza Atrium, Kuala Lumpur, 1984.
Ken Yeang/T. R. Hamzah & Yeang.

Fig. 3.19 Plaza Atrium, Ken Yeang/T. R. Hamzah & Yeang.

Fig. 3.20 IBM Plaza, Kuala Lumpur, 1987.
Ken Yeang/T. R. Hamzah & Yeang.

Fig. 3.21 Menara Mesiniaga, Subang Jaya, near Kuala Lumpur, 1992. Ken Yeang/T. R. Hamzah & Yeang.

Fig. 3.22 MBf Tower, Penang, 1994. Ken Yeang/
T. R. Hamzah & Yeang.

Fig. 3.23 Hitechniaga Headquarters, tower proposal, 1995.
Ken Yeang/T. R. Hamzah & Yeang.

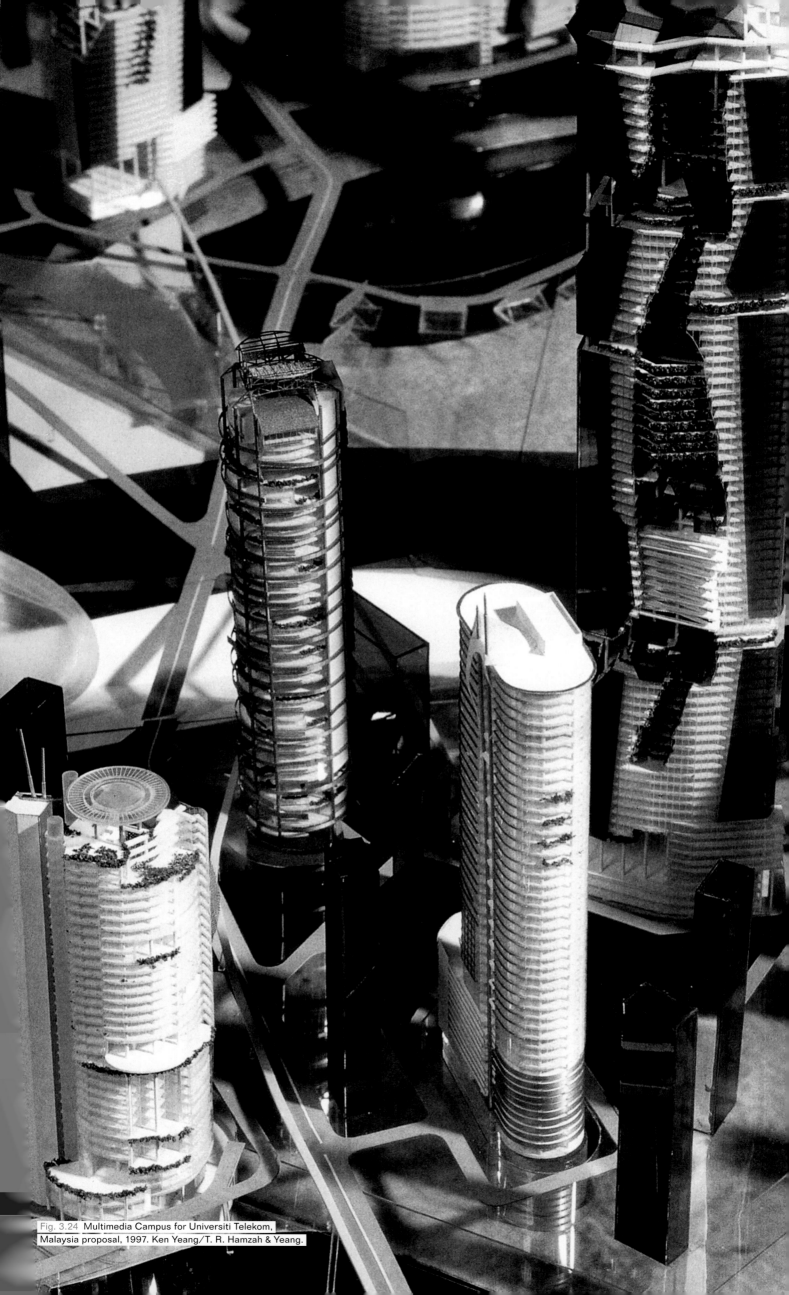

Fig. 3.24 Multimedia Campus for Universiti Telekom,
Malaysia proposal, 1997. Ken Yeang/T. R. Hamzah & Yeang.

Fig. 3.25 Waterfront Tower, proposal, Kuala Lumpur, 2004.
Ken Yeang/T. R. Hamzah & Yeang.

Chapter 4

Designer Skyscraper

The Environmental Skyscraper
The Enrichment
of Vertical Space
Inevitable
Skyscraper

New Yorkers had barely closed their calendars on the last millennium when full-page advertisements in the Sunday *New York Times* featured two startling new residential towers. Fig. 4.1 173 and 176 Perry Street, two white-framed glass towers available for occupancy in 2002, stood out against the familiar brick hodge-podge of West Greenwich Village. Rumors circulated that early residents included Martha Stewart, Nicole Kidman, Calvin Klein and Brad Pitt, and led to a prompt pre-opening closeout of all of the first tower's units. Although sales were surprisingly brisk even by Manhattan standards, several factors helped propel the success of these new apartments.

The buildings were designed by Richard Meier in a style that could be characterized as only his. Neo-modern, pure and Corbusian, Meier's transparent prisms could not have appeared in more contrast to the neighborhood's intimate scale of close streets, eclectic brick buildings and low rooflines. Fig. 4.2 They appeared to represent an altogether different paradigm of residence in this historic neighborhood, though they were sited hard by the Westside Highway, availing them of broad views beyond the Village and out across the Hudson River. Fig. 4.3

All advertisements for the property, and promotional news articles that followed featured Meier prominently. His international status, his Pritzker Prize and his recent completion of the Getty Museum commission in California were front and center in media and marketing. As the projects extended the visual legacy of much of Meier's previous work, and he was by this time widely recognized, the buildings and Richard Meier were, in a new way, presented, and by all accounts, perceived to be one and the same.

The initial images of the project displayed the striking exteriors reflected in a setting sun against a backdrop of the brooding historic city, but over time, advertisements, news articles, and particularly features in architectural magazines, began to reveal a vision of the interiors. Stark, empty, wrapped in floor-to-ceiling glass without window coverings, these images would occasionally display minimal modern furniture to establish scale or suggest some domestic purpose. While savvy marketers of luxury projects have always understood the wealthy resident's affinity for retail consumption, they have generally responded by featuring in sales literature interior images of a life of acquisition. These interiors were presented, by contrast, as spare, even ascetic.

Furthermore, the legendary real estate mantra "location, location, location" appeared to be upended. Located downtown, beyond an easy walk to subway lines, at the edge of small streets facing out across the busy Westside Highway, and certainly not in an established and fashionable area, identifiable by wide tree-lined streets and gentrified properties, the new towers seemed to succeed upon another kind of premise. The iconic and minimalist towers formed an alternative paradigm, one more closely allied with contemporary modern art whereby the joint facts of a pedigree and a questionable location established their credibility. Rather like a trip to a museum, a gallery or an installation to see works by a particular artist, a certain kind of art-smart consumer appeared more than willing to venture out into unfamiliar corners of the city to behold this particular phenomenon. This phenomenon was a place to live, and it would be, like the artwork, a destination.

Although other residential tower projects had been in the works, and boutique hotels for some years had offered guests a "complete" designer experience, 173 and 176 Perry Street crystallized a kind of success new to the residential building type. This particular and complete experience projected a young and pioneering vibe (location), a modern and cutting-edge attitude (minimalist modern architecture), and a high art affiliation (an interior suited for the display of modern art). In order to achieve an evermore complete experience, Meier not only designed all interior finishes, but offered "total design

services" to residents who wished to have additional finishes, window coverings and furnishings installed to fully discharge the intent of the designer. Plentiful wall-long closets were provided, enabling residents to realize Meier's minimal, uncluttered vision. A long list of concierge services were made available to both supplement upscale survival in this border location as well as to fully amenitize the simple life.

At last count, some 15,000 new high-rise residential units were on the market in Manhattan, certainly more than in any other American city. While a wide range of product is available, there has always been a strong sales trend in New York City for historically inclined buildings, ones epitomizing tradition, a heritage and a kind of decorative taste. Fig. 4.4 Robert Stern's 15 Central Park West, an updated recall of the city's grand pre-war limestone buildings, and the Brompton on East Eighty-Fifth Street are conveyed to market with terms like "stylishly proper" and "a return to elegance." Michael Graves' personalized classicism pervades the Impala and 425 Fifth Avenue, and Peter Marino has newly weighed in with a solid dose of the past in his East End Avenue cooperative apartments. Building conversions have always been a staple in New York, and none shouts history like the new hotel residences at the Plaza, where we are beckoned to "own the legend."

Still, it appears that modernism has a new benefactor in the real estate development community as it becomes the style of choice for new residential skyscrapers. While little compares to New York for dense and competitively marketed construction, the spill-over effect is easily observed in South Florida, Las Vegas, Chicago, Los Angeles and, to varying degrees, other cities that are strong urban residential markets.

It has by now gone well-noticed that in addition to the resurrection of a latent modernism, a seamless conflation has been affected between designer identity and the world of retail. More precisely, and relevant to the skyscraper now, not only are the social mechanics of luxury goods being used to inform architecture, but architecture is conversely informing the design and marketing of luxury products. Through a widely publicized process of international competitions, prizes and periodicals, and with the frequently strong support of academia, architects and their output have become the equivalent of European luxury brands. Real estate organizations consider themselves fundamentally retail operations, trade to an exclusive clientele, and commonly commission architects of a standing they consider to be equal to the aspiration of their product. Flagship fashion boutiques, museums, galleries, specialized hotels and spas, landmark office buildings and now, residential towers are all appropriating willing architects in an effort to transform culture into retail. The current trend seems so well established that the long list of architectural sightings is well established and continues to expand: Kazuyo Sejima featured among the advertising pages of *Vogue* magazine, Zaha Hadid's latest handbag design for Louis Vuitton in *W*, and Frank Gehry's jewelry line for Tiffany. Even Los Angeles' Museum of Contemporary Art's 2006 blockbuster "Skin + Bones" exhibition matched up high fashion and architecture with an equivalence that had both quarters presumably gaining prestige through association.

Andrea Schwann, a publicist for the luxury real estate industry, notes, "It's no accident that the condo market parallels the art market. Strategies of luxury branding that used to sell Lanvin and Gucci were applied to condominium architecture."[1] Richard Pandiscio, former creative director of *Interview* magazine and longtime collaborator of hotelier André Balazs, brings a background in the worlds of fashion, art and design to bear on his promotional activities in real estate. In a recent *New York Times* article, Pandiscio is said to be "trying to sell you not just an apartment, but a piece of history, a dream, an identity."[2] The Urban Glass House, a new high-rise residence he marketed in Soho carries the tag line, "modernist luxury has evolved." Fig. 4.5 Recalling Philip Johnson's 1949 iconic glass house in New Canaan, Connecticut, this twelve-story glass tower Fig. 4.6 takes some of the simplicity of its window wall from the straightforward lines of the original, but more than any physical resemblance, the building, and the sales narrative, are used to recall the universe of highly pedigreed luxury *objets* from the mid-century modern period: marketing parties at Johnson's Four Seasons restaurant, a sales catalogue with an introduction to modernism written by Britain's prized critic Deyan Sudjic, museum gift shop bags finished in black-and-white Lucite. Space in the building is modern, historical, artistic, luxurious, exclusive, and now, immediately available. "Live in an instant landmark," Pandiscio promises. Irrespective of the building's status as architecture, it clearly triggers the recognition of sophistication in the minds of strategically informed consumers.

What is apparent in examining the New York condition is that due to its geographic limitations and highly competitive market, prices for residential real estate in the city have increased nearly fifty percent in five years. More than thirty percent of all for-sale apartments are other than primary residences, that is to say, investments and second homes. Certain designer-branded residential towers fetch twenty-five to fifty percent premiums over generic comparables. All these conditions demonstrate what an economist would call an upward-tending supply and demand curve, with the ability to identify an ultra-premium market niche at the top end. In short, a bracing market exists. Significant monies appear to be made by collecting, holding and selling high-end residences. Like other collectibles such as stocks, fine art and wine inventories, residences in landmark towers, too, become commodities: purchased, held and sold for an appreciated value.

The work of Jean Nouvel, France's accomplished 64-year-old architect, exemplifies the trend. Invited into the high-stakes design game of New York's residential marketplace, Nouvel was commissioned by André Balazs to design a twelve-story tower in the heart of Soho's fine arts and retail district. The building recalls, in an elegant and contemporary way, the cast-iron structures of the neighborhood's industrial past. Updated, with a nod to the classic elegance of Mies van der Rohe's 1951 Lakeshore Drive residential towers in Chicago and the nearer Seagram Building, the residence's exterior is a taut cage of slate grey steel members framing wide expanses of glass, and set back at the fifth floor in response to the scale of older masonry-and-iron buildings on the street. Fig. 4.7 – Fig. 4.8 The experience of the tower, at all scales, is much more emotive and wry than it's precedents. The ground-floor entry lobby is dramatically narrow and tall with large reflective panels depicting forested black and white images. Lighting is low, drawing one's attention to a slot of glass in the floor, allowing a glimpse to the basement pool below, shimmering in aqueous light. Narrow horizontal bands laid into the otherwise unadorned glass window wall reflect deep blue and red tones into the apartments, while oversized and mechanized exterior glass panels drop down to transform living areas into covered terraces. This elegant conceit allows the building to both be experienced as an elaborate Post-Corbusian machine (in the spirit of Nouvel's earlier Nemausus housing project in Nîmes and his L'Institut du Monde Arabe in Paris) and to appear to spill the intimate contents of the residences out into public view.

Nouvel's second building in New York is the twenty-two-story residential tower in Chelsea, next to Frank Gehry's InterActiveCorporation (IAC) building. The north and east facing elevations, which give onto inner property lines, are composed of rough black concrete blocks punctured erratically by windows of varying sizes. Facing out to the Hudson and the IAC building, the west and southern elevations contain 1650 window panes set in steel frames and composed of multiple window modules, varying both in size and in tilt. Tinted and coated, the windows will reflect the sky and surrounding landscape in a glistening wall of multiple reflections. Fig. 4.9 Once again, like Meier's original buildings just south on the Westside Highway, the faceted skyscraper asserts its highly designed self as an artful destination in an emerging neighborhood. A large sign-board on site provides contact information to prospective buyers in the form of www.nouvelchelsea.com.

Jean Nouvel's third and latest commission in New York City is the design of another luxury residential high-rise, an addition to the Museum of Modern Art complex on West Fifty-Fourth Street. Following a highly promoted competition including Diller Scofidio + Renfro, Morphosis, Reiser and Umamoto, and Nicholas Grimshaw, Nouvel was selected to design a second tower to follow the recent museum expansion. This time, the design included a sixty-plus-story high-rise on a base of 75,000 square feet of additional exhibition and speculative office space. Coming after the discrete and tenta-tive expansion by Yoshio Taniguchi, the new building will be doubly branded, conveying MOMA's institutional identity and Nouvel's penchant for experimentation.

The designer branding of residential towers has become widespread. In New York City alone, buildings by Santiago Calatrava, Bernard Tschumi, Enrique Norten, Charles Gwathmey, Norman Foster, Christian de Portzamparc, Philippe Starck, SHoP Architects, Asymptote and David Rockwell, to name only a few, crowd city neighborhoods. Fig. 4.10 – Fig. 4.11 Most of these are sleek late-modern monoliths developers believe can be priced higher than comparable properties without designer status. In an extreme example, Calatrava's 80 South Street tower, spiraling heavenward but consisting of only twelve self-contained residences, if built, will fetch $29 million each. Fig. 4.12 – Fig. 4.13

High Hospitality

Ian Schrager, the boutique hotel impresario, has had much to do with recent trends in vertical hospitality buildings. Gaining a footing in the industry with his business partner at the time, Steve Rubell, Schrager founded the enormously successful New York City night clubs Studio 54 and Palladium in the late 1970s and '80s. Following a respite from the club life, he opened a string of small specialty hotels in existing historic towers known for the social energy of their common spaces and the

unique design identities he gave them with the support of cult designers such as Andrée Putman and Philippe Starck. Through each hotel's marriage of unique design and social cachet, these boutique operations have attracted both locals and out-of-town guests. In New York, Schrager developed Morgans, the Royalton and the Paramount, moving on to the Delano in Miami's South Beach, the Clift in San Francisco, the Mondrian in West Hollywood, and back to New York City for the Hudson. Recently, he has chosen to develop joint residential and hotel properties in order to co-brand the two and provide reciprocal services and amenities.

At 50 Gramercy Park North and the Gramercy Park Hotel, Schrager commis-sioned the English architect, John Pawson, to design a sleek minimalist residential tower with enormous windows of floor-to-ceiling glass, giving onto Gramercy Park. At the hotel, the artist, Julian Schnabel, was select-ed by Schrager to provide an altogether different sensibility of bohemian cool, a multi-colored interior design of rich, moody and highly eccentric spaces, a foil to the residential building. While the two stand stylistically apart, they work together as a lifestyle program. Round-the-clock access to all Gramercy Park Hotel services and amenities is ensured to residents, as is apartment oversight, supervision, administra-tion, management and care, something curiously termed in the sales literature as "lifestyle management." Catering, car care, butler valet and personal shopping services, apartment renovation and repair, membership in the hotel gym and spa, and priority status for hotel room and restaurant reservations are guaranteed.

On the level of cross-marketing, this pairing of related building types, frequently stacked vertically in a tall building, is advantageous to many of the customers who choose to purchase such residences. Frequently, more limited by time than money, these consumers prefer a broad set of convenient services nearby or in the building, if properly matched to their preferences. Many similarly con-ceived projects, in cities such as New York where the only available development sites are no longer central but in transitional neighborhoods, need to be reasonably self-sufficient due to a dearth of nearby services, neighborhood safety and security issues and limited transportation options. All of these factors are coalescing now to create a new hotel-with-branded residences building type which is both vertical and mixed-use.

Schrager recently completed a second luxury residential building further downtown. Fig. 4.17 40 Bond contains only twenty-seven residences, and has been co-branded with its not-so-near sibling, the Gramercy Park

Hotel. The building, designed by Jacques Herzog and Pierre de Meuron, in yet another unique and contemporary style, is sold with similar access and services provided by Gramercy Park Hotel management, although its location is just off a vibrant commercial street where retail services are widely available.

This twenty-year boutique trend has transformed a significant portion of the hospitality and residential markets. In 2007, Schrager and Marriott International, one of the world's largest hotel companies, announced that they had entered an agreement to design and develop jointly 100 boutique hotels throughout the world. Schrager will design the concepts, a third-party developer in each location will develop and construct the building, and Marriott will operate each. Any plans to include and co-brand residential components have not been disclosed. While Marriott has $12 billion in annual sales worldwide through its nearly 3,000 properties, the company is visibly absent in the boutique category. In a growing overall hospitality market, the boutiques are the single fastest growing segment. Starwood's W Hotels, Morgans Hotel Group, Kor Hotel Group, Joie de Vivre, Kimpton Hotels, André Balazs Properties and Thompson Hotels are among the many expanding in this area.

As boutique concepts are reproduced and mainstreamed, we can expect to see a multitude of these mixed-use urban buildings each differentiated in idiosyncratic and highly mannered ways, appealing to broader markets in a wider range of geographic locations. Anna Wintour, editor of *Vogue* magazine, believes that this is part of a larger trend in the fashion world. Citing other commercial collaborations, such as designers Vera Wang for Kohl's and Isaac Mizrahi for Target, Wintour states that "more and more people are working within the mainstream."[3] Calvin Klein describes the new marriage in its most optimistic light: "Marriott has the resources and infrastructure to manage a global brand, while Ian has the ability to create it."[4]

Variations

The marketability of the designer brand for tall residential buildings has moved well beyond New York. In Los Angeles, Frank Gehry's design for the first phase of a multi-block project for New York's Related Companies includes a forty-eight-story Mandarin Oriental Hotel, topped with luxury condos. Though the design is preliminary, the tower has been presented as sheathed in reflective glass to the exterior with inside surfaces exhibiting the structural grid of the building covered in large-scale pictorial

images of vegetation. Fig. 4.15 Live oak trees and lush landscaping grow out of the tops of the towers. These treatments suggest that the building will be sufficiently unique and identifiably Gehryesque, to the point of being an extension of his brand and a signifier of the new breed of designer hotel/residences. Notwithstanding outdated community guidelines, which continue to discourage highly reflective glass buildings or supergraphics, Gehry is reintroducing these visual effects, post-Guggenheim Bilbao and post-Disney Hall, in a world populated by large-scale images made relevant again by the work of artists like Bill Viola and Doug Aitken.

While Los Angeles' limited history of residential towers has been largely undistinguished, and a significant conversion of existing buildings downtown to new residences is underway, a number of new buildings are now being designed by well-known national architects whose bodies of work distinguish the projects. The verdict is out, however, as to whether the overall market for high-end residential towers in Los Angeles will become large enough such that designer towers will achieve the kind of status required to become collectible and traded.

The modern designer-brand is returning to Chicago, the birthplace of the skyscraper. Home to Mies van der Rohe's 860 and 880 Lake Shore Drive, Bertrand Goldberg's Marina City, and Bruce Graham and Fazlur Khan's 1450-foot-tall Sears Tower, many new tall building projects appear to have the presence to distinguish themselves. Like most American cities, Chicago's office market crashed in the early 1990s. In response, the City Planning Department thereafter began to encourage residential density in an attempt to supplement the high office vacancies and establish a 24/7 level of activity in the Loop and to the north. Following that, a series of unremarkable buildings appeared, prompting a 2003 article in the *Chicago Sun-Times* by Mayor Richard M. Daley, headlined: "No More Ugly Buildings." Real estate developers faced the prospect that the city of historic patronage would either only support better building or perhaps make undistinguished buildings difficult to entitle. A new and rigorous energy code was adopted and a recent spate of tall residential projects suggests that distinctively modern towers may again be a hallmark of Chicago.

The Chicago Spire, designed by Santiago Calatrava in association with DeStefano + Partners is certainly the most iconic of the city's many proposals. At 124 floors, the building's 2000-foot-height would overtake the Sears Tower as the city's tallest building. In the spirit of his Turning Torso in Malmö, Sweden, and his 80 South Street in

Manhattan, Calatrava proposes a tapering and tortile tower of glass that includes 300 residences over a base of 150 hotel rooms. Since its design, the project whose completion date is unknown, has been sold and awaits even more consumer demand in the high-end housing market. Murphy/Jahn's first high-rise residential structure in Chicago, 600 North Fairbanks, tops out at forty-one stories. An all-glass building, the tower is a simple vertical extrusion, with a smooth curve at the exposed corner of the site and an open frame at the top.

The Seattle, Washington-based Miller Hull Partnership presents its starkly modern brand of industrial architecture in a mini-tower of eleven dwellings known simply as 156 West Superior. Fig. 4.19 Expressing its steel facade, diagonal bracing and projecting balconies, the building recalls Mies van der Rohe's earlier infatuation with structural-steel sections, yet presents it in a rough, yet elegantly organized, composition. One of the most dramatic and curious of the new towers is Aqua by Studio Gang Architects, an eighty-one-story building already being copied for its iconic effects produced with an efficiency of means. A hotel/condo, the tower is a simple rectangle draped with an undulating series of balconies wrapping the building. Fig. 4.18 Between its name, the ripples of its exterior and the effects of night lighting, the building achieves a shimmering image of what is, in fact, a simple rectangular monolith.

Miami's version of the same building is called Regalia on Collins Avenue. The same device produces a similar effect. This time the ripples resonate in a city known for the ocean beach nearby. A large number of ocean-view condos have gone up or are being marketed in South Florida, the land of the second home, many of them modern, from One Thousand Ocean at the Boca Resort & Beach Club and Chad Oppenheim's proposed Cube, Fig. 4.14 to 9449 Collins Avenue. Sited on the home of the former Beach House Hotel, this condominium project is touted as the "Beach House Designed by Richard Meier," and promises to be nothing less than the life and mind of the architect.

At last count, there were more than eighty building permits for high-rise buildings in Las Vegas, most of them residences in a second land of the second home, in this case, a land with extremely favorable tax laws. Las Vegas' characteristic penchant for building bigger, harnessing unnatural events like the installation of forested mountains and sand beaches in the middle of the desert, and the omnipresence of luxury retail along the most minor of circulation corridors, places these buildings into a genre of their own. The Tower, at the Beach Club, developed for the Global Hyatt Corporation, advertises "urban

indulgence," which marketing literature breaks into nine apparently essential program elements: *The Beach Club, The Casino, The Shops, The Playground, The Dining Club, The Spa, The Fitness Center, The Theater, The Night Club*

Entitled The Cosmopolitan Resort & Casino, the project literature describes an urban tower strategically redefined by elements it considers to make up the urban "Las Vegas Style" and appealing to buyers with a surfeit of time on their hands and an appetite for stimulation. The everyday questions Americans ask elsewhere when considering how and where to live such as the locations of markets and schools and proximity to work, friends and healthcare, have been drained out of the purchasing equation here. The buyer confronts the residential tower solely as a luxury item.

Peter Morton's recently unveiled expansion of Las Vegas' Hard Rock Hotel involves five towers, all of strikingly minimalist modern design. Further expanding his original brand from cafés to hotels and now to high-rise residences, Morton has followed the purchasing path of a class of aging, and wealthy, baby boomers. Pure modernist forms clad primarily in glass, the towers are sited in a lush tropical landscape. Chad Oppenheim, the New York architect, recalling his fantasy high-rise proposals for Miami, has been commissioned to design these 1,200 units of high-rise condominiums, condo-hotel rooms and poolside bungalows. In the condo-hotel format, or "condotel," the residential units are rented out on a short-term basis for the benefit of their owners, in a cross between a traditional condominium and a timeshare. This type of development has its roots in Miami and San Diego and is now extending into Hawaii and Las Vegas, locations which serve as vacation sites in a format that reduces the buyer's total costs.

By any measure, the most formidable entry into the Las Vegas wars for the new residential buyer, is what has been called CityCenter, a multibillion dollar, sixty-seven-acre development on the Strip. Fig. 4.16 The project development and hospitality company, MGM MIRAGE, commissioned a raft of well-known architects including Rafael Vinoly, Helmut Jahn, Norman Foster, Cesar Pelli and Kohn Pedersen Fox Architects, to design the multitude of buildings that will sit between the Monte Carlo and Bellagio hotels. Comprising eighteen million square feet, the size of Rockefeller Center, Times Square and SOHO combined, the master plan was created by Stan Eckstut, planner for New York's Battery Park City. Replete with markets and retail services, Eckstut explains, "It will be a real urban district of variety and complexity that borrows from traditional cities … walking is stressed throughout."[5] CityCenter, with its designer residences, its promise of a mix of services and pedestrian access, will demonstrate, in a project of this enormity, whether newness and a lack of history can successfully simulate a spontaneous urban place.

In a world of tall buildings as commercial brands, communications loom large. Naming becomes paramount. It is interesting and informative to observe how project names and individual names are associated either for benefit to the project or for benefit to the individual name brand. The least nuanced is, perhaps, the tall building by Trump: Trump Tower, Trump Palace, Trump Parc, Trump Grande and Trump Ocean Club International. As the buildings tend toward the generic, so does the naming. In "Trumpworld," the identity of the architect, as well as the specific details of the projects, are down-played in pursuit of a simplification and an immediate reinforcement of the Trump brand: big, omnipresent, gleaming and affluent.

A grayer area seems to be staked out by Ian Schrager in his many boutique properties. Originally marketed as Morgans Hotel or the Royalton or Paramount, the name Schrager was very much a byline in advertising the early properties. As the brand spread geo-graphically and became more recognizable, with price points rising, additional projects began to be identified as the Schrager Clift Hotel, the Schrager Delano and the Schrager Hudson. As he now pursues the integration of luxury hotels and residences, he has chosen to jointly identify the properties by location and his own creative identity, assigning the names of design architects to an important but secondary role. While the architect John Pawson was featured in early announcements for 50 Gramercy Park North, and Herzog & de Meuron featured for 40 Bond, successfully confirming the projects as designer products, the name Schrager subsequently overtook the literature. Whereas San Francisco's De Young Museum issues self-effacing retail bags boldly stating "A Herzog and de Meuron Museum," the headlines for Schrager's properties make his role clear: "City Living Reinvented by Ian Schrager" and, simply, "Home by Ian Schrager." Perhaps by elevating the Shrager name over those of the property or the designers, the brand can have its own life and be transferred successfully to the new Marriott venture.

As established neighborhoods are built out and new projects search for more outlying sites, certain properties attempt to over-come the perceived deficit of a transitional neighborhood through naming. Tribeca's 101 Warren Street has gamely referred to itself as "101 Pine Tree Forest" in early advertisements, underscoring the sponsor's intent to plant one hundred and one pine trees at the ground level, in a neighborhood known for its historically industrial character and lack of green open space. "Enjoy a farmstand every day of your life" and "Whole Foods Market at your doorstep" have also led the sales literature. These slogans worked to replace the perception of Tribeca's lack of grocery venues with the promise of an urban farmer's market. Following that, bylines exist for the design-ers: "Architecture by Skidmore, Owings & Merrill," "Interior Décor by Victoria Hagan" or "Landscape Design by Thomas Balsley."

While it can be argued that the skyscraper has always been a prestigious commercial icon bought and sold, it has seldom before been described in the intimate terms we associate with personal consumption and elite authorship. The cult of the designer skyscraper has never been stronger nor grown faster than in the residential market-place. From headlines such as 15 Central Park West's "Designed By Robert A.M. Stern", to Brooklyn's "Richard Meier On Prospect Park" and Tribeca's "One York Enrique Norten," the tower, the designer and the prospect of ownership have become inseparable. Fig. 4.20

Notes

[1] Giovannini, Joseph, *The Evolution of Development: NY*, Form, op. cit., 52.

[2] Browne, Alix, *Spin City*, The New York Times Magazine, October 9, 2005, Talk, op. cit., 88.

[3] Stodghill, Ron, *A Hotelier Is Breaking The Mold Once Again*, The New York Times, Sunday Business, op. cit. 8.

[4] ibid., 8

[5] Pogrebin, Robin, *"A New City Center for Las Vegas,"* The New York Times, September 15, 2005, B1.

Fig. 4.1 Perry Street Condominiums, New York City, 2002.
Richard Meier & Partners.

Fig. 4.2 Perry Street Condominiums and Charles
Street Condominiums, New York City, 2006.
Richard Meier & Partners

Fig. 4.3 Balcony detail, Perry Street Condominiums.
Richard Meier & Partners.

Fig. 4.4 Central Park West, New York City, 2006.

Fig. 4.5 The Urban Glass House, billboard, New York City, 2006.

Fig. 4.6 **The Urban Glass House, model.**
Philip Johnson and Annabelle Selldorf.

Fig. 4.7 40 Mercer Residences, living room, New York City, 2008.
Ateliers Jean Nouvel.

Fig. 4.8 40 Mercer Residences, penthouse. Ateliers Jean Nouvel

160

Fig. 4.10 75 Wall Street rooftop, New York City, 2008. Rockwell Group.

Fig. 4.11 BLUE Residential Tower, New York City, 2007.
Bernard Tschumi Architects.

Fig. 4.12 80 South Street rendering, New York City, 2008.
Santiago Calatrava.

Fig. 4.13 80 South Street. Santiago Calatrava.

Fig. 4.14 "Cube: Life Unstructured – Custom Home
Possibilities In the Sky", Miami, 2008. Chad Oppenheim.

Fig. 4.15 The Grand model, Los Angeles, 2008.
Gehry Partners.

Fig. 4.16 CityCenter, rendering, Las Vegas, 2008. Murphy/
Jahn Architects, Rafael Viñoly Architects, Foster + Partners,
Kohn Pedersen Fox Associates, Pelli Clarke Pelli Architects,
Studio Daniel Libeskind, Rockwell Group, Gensler.

Fig. 4.17 40 Bond rendering, New York City, 2008.
Herzog & de Meuron.

Fig. 4.18 Aqua Tower, Chicago, 2009. Studio Gang Architects.

Fig. 4.19 156 West Superior, Chicago, 2006.
Miller Hull Partnership.

ONE YORK ENRIQUE NORTEN

Fig. 4.20 One York, New York City, 2008.
Enrique Norten/TEN Arquitectos.

Chapter 5

FutureTall

Designer
Skyscraper
The Environmental
Skyscraper
The Enrichment
of Vertical Space
Inevitable
Skyscraper

Perhaps no medium we can think of portrays more strikingly the surreal impact tall buildings can have on the developing world, and the kind of visual anomie that unites both its slums and its advantaged urban areas, than the urban photography of Thomas Struth. Fig. 5.3 In emerging countries, where the skyscraper can be the ultimate signifier of sophistication, economic advantage, even opulence, it also carries with it the contradictory power to convey a muddled sense of urgency and banality. Growing communities in Asia and the Middle East, are constructing tall buildings at a rate and to heights which far outstrip the pace and scale of similar development in the highly industrialized West.

Asia

Until twenty years ago, most tall buildings in Asia were located in Japan and Hong Kong. Post-World War II rebuilding efforts in a number of major Japanese cities represented early efforts to increase density and establish a modern legacy of tall buildings. In Hong Kong, one of the great yet geographically constrained commercial centers of Asia, tall buildings had long been the norm for office buildings, hotels and residences.

Here, the demand for high-rise residences alone has historically been so high that the Western paradigm of the freestanding modern tower as a unique architectural object has given way to the tower as a part of the urban background. In Hong Kong, each apartment tower typically appears as one of a blanket of tall buildings, similar for the common economic logic of its floor plan and its regulated uniform building height. In fact, it is common today in Hong Kong for single projects to include as many as thirty multi-story towers comprising several thousand residences. Few cities, even in areas of explosive growth, exhibit such intense demand and repetition. Fig. 5.6

Japan has trod its own unique path in pursuit of the ultimate skyscraper. Whereas tall buildings and dense infill are typical in major cities throughout post-war Japan, a number of huge multi-use projects in central Tokyo characterize ongoing trends in the application of scale and program. Mirroring the monolithic and far-reaching power of major Japanese corporations to operate successfully within their own business environment, and their phenomenal growth and tendency toward internalizing ownership, skyscrapers have become bigger than ever, incorporating destination shopping centers, cultural facilities, hospitality and major landscape improvements into vast programs. Projects most exemplary of this trend have come on line in recent years, following the bursting of the "bubble economy" in the early 1990s. As a result of the need for many corporations to correct balance sheets and massively divest, as well as the multiple land auctions the national government sponsored due to bankruptcies, major Japanese real estate companies have been able to assemble and purchase large areas of urban land at attractive prices.

In an attempt to keep up with competing non-Japanese markets, Tokyo has been preparing to create world-class business centers to take on the challenge posed by locations such as Singapore and Shanghai. Japanese commercial environments that attract international business travel, destination tourism and luxury retail are typically synthesized into mega-centers anchored by skyscrapers. In many specific ways, the metropolitan government encourages this privately driven development trend through its support of land assembly, entitlement and building permits. The details of Tokyo's favorable disposition toward real estate development are outlined in the "2001 New City Planning Vision for Tokyo," a document that describes the challenges of a metropolitan area which comprises some 30 million people, many of whom commute two to three hours per day. As a result, the plan calls for increasing density in the central districts by adding vertical infill building and mixed-use services in an effort to reduce demand on a regional transportation system that is currently running at 150 percent of its design capacity.[1]

These multi-million-square-foot skyscraper projects, such as Roppongi Hills, Fig. 5.1 Tokyo Midtown, Shiodome, Omotesando Hills and the Shin-Marunouchi Building, are all multi-year planning projects, created by Japan's largest and most powerful business conglomerates, among them, Mori Building, Mitsui Fudosan and Mitsubishi Estate.

Roppongi Hills, developed by Mori Building, also responsible for the Shanghai World Financial Center in Pudong, is located in a typical Tokyo ward known for its modest shops, restaurants and bars. The project has recreated an entire neighborhood through the introduction of the usual mix of high-rise office, hotel, housing and retail services. Designed by a vast team that included KPF, the Jerde Partnership, Fumihiko Maki and Terence Conran, the project supplements its commercial elements with a wide range of public and semi-public venues. The skyscraper component of the overall master plan is no exception: the top floors feature a roof deck with publicly accessible viewing facilities, Fig. 5.2 the Mori Art Museum and the Roppongi Hills Club, and a hospitality institution that provides free membership to international diplomats. Below these are located the Mori Urban Institute for the Future, a private research and exhibition gallery that publishes literature on world cities, and the Roppongi Hills Academy, an interactive and multi-functional education center open to the public. These facilities, while undoubtedly business-friendly and beneficial in distinguishing Roppongi Hills in a highly competitive real estate market, elevate the importance of cultural and educational resources within a commercial tower and privilege them symbolically by placing many of them near the top of the tower, a location both visible and customarily capable of returning the highest rents.

Architecturally, while highly finished and detailed, the extra-large Roppongi Hills office tower has no neighbors of commensurate scale on the immediate skyline. Not even its own twin residential towers serve to mediate its height and girth with the diminutive scale of the pre-existing surroundings. While the public programming of the tower's top floors is surprising, the most architecturally inventive spaces are at the project's swirling and highly pedestrianized base. Curving limestone trays of single-loaded shopping, heavily landscaped roofs, and Maki's carefully crafted TV Asahi headquarters make up a slick jumble of forms that mirrors the eccentric roadways, trapezoidal buildings, and architectural odds and ends at the perimeter of the site.

The latest entry in this uniquely Japanese field, Tokyo Midtown, makes a reference, one supposes, to Manhattan's own Midtown, for its attractive blend of sophisticated corporate work environments and luxury retail space. Fig. 5.4 – Fig 5.5 Designed by New York architect David Childs and SOM, the project may be a New York "wanna-be," but lacks the spontaneity and historic patina that characterizes a Madison or Fifth Avenue. A brand-spanking new ensemble of hyper-gridded buildings, anchored by an office and hotel tower, the most compelling part of the project is once again the ground plane, which opens up to generous landscaping and an extraordinary art gallery by Tadao Ando, still managing to mirror the eccentric little through-block passages and retail galleries that populate so much of the city.

Finally, a project which opened at the same time as Tokyo Midtown, the Shin-Marunouchi Building, is a simple point tower by the British architect Michael Hopkins, and is representative of the more typical players in the field. With ground-level (or near ground-level) retail so valuable in Tokyo, one enters the project at the sidewalk, to discover a retail basement level below and seven shopping levels above. Atop those are approximately thirty floors of undifferentiated and highly efficient office floor plates. The program is conventional and, while the detailing is immaculate, the building is a rather highly finished high-performance office leasing machine.

In China, now that laws have been rewritten to allow private ownership of improved property, much of the dense high-rise development of today's commercial centers is buoyed by a profusion of towers. The scale of these projects tends toward the enormous, whether single buildings, such as Beijing's 2.4-million-square-foot China World Trade Center Tower, or multi-building centers, like Shanghai's 17 million square foot Brilliant City. Tall buildings are being built across the country in cities scarcely known to Westerners and boasting populations in the many millions: Guangzhou, Shenzhen, Dalian, Chongqing and Chengdu. Outlying regional centers like Singapore, Makati City and Manila in the Philippines, Seoul, Incheon and Pusan in South Korea, Kuala Lumpur in Malaysia and Indonesia's Jakarta, all compete to be the home of the world's tallest buildings.

The development of skyscrapers, like all things Western, began slowly in China. Contacts and trade with outside countries failed to occur until the middle of the nineteenth century. For centuries prior, the sheer size, geographic barriers and presence of a central state, had kept China culturally isolated and insular. Increasingly, Christian missionaries and foreign traders penetrated the country, bringing with them more effective weaponry, industrial tools, education,

a culture of management and transportation. In 1842, European forces were successful in getting China to relinquish Hong Kong and five other treaty ports for the purpose of establishing interface between themselves and the Chinese. These port cities were located on the coastal fringes of China's Middle Kingdom far from the Imperial Court in Beijing.

With the fall of the emperor and the founding of the Republic of China in 1911, Sun Yat-sen became China's first president. His nationalist semi-democratic government, while still feudal in its operations, further encouraged Western exchange. Traditional culture changed little for the masses. The ruling and wealthy merchant classes absorbed much of the protocols, dress, business and recreational customs of their new Western trading partners.

In 1949, when the People's Republic of China was established, it largely adopted the Soviet Union's socialist model of governance, which included concerns regarding appropriate "national form" and building technology. The tentative relationship between China and the Soviet Union failed, however, in the 1960s, when the two countries clashed over ideology. By 1978, when China implemented its Open Door Policy, overseas trade and global communications gained access to the general culture. For many Chinese, the prospect of Western architecture spawned a debate about the correctness of traditional Chinese forms versus European modernism, symbolizing the technologically advanced and commercialized West. In some circles, this continues to be a vigorous and protracted exchange today.

It was at this juncture, that several hotels were designed and built that became the opening gambit in the Western building campaign that was soon to follow. In Beijing, I.M. Pei's 1982 Fragrant Hill Hotel represented the first building designed by a "foreigner," and one that attempted to mediate modernism with a sense of classic Chinese history. Following that, a series of very Western style high-rise hotels were created, which both set a standard for comfortably accommodating international trade as well as inserting an identifiable brand of modernism into Chinese commercial life. Palmer & Turner's 1983 Jin Lin Hotel in Nanjing at thirty-seven-stories became an instant icon with a reputation for the highest level of service available in the region. In the same year, Ellerbe Becket's eighteen-story Great Wall Hotel in Beijing represented the first glass curtain wall building in China. Fig. 5.7

Other tall buildings designed by Western architects appeared as their Chinese sponsors began to travel widely and admire the architecture, the technical quality of Western buildings and the kinds of cultural and commercial institutions that were created abroad. In 1989, John Portman's Shanghai Centre was modeled after his Peachtree Center in Atlanta and Bonaventure Hotel in Los Angeles: central atrium wrapped with a mixed-use podium plus hotel towers rising above. Fig. 5.8 The architecture was straightforward and the model of a Western-style mixed-use high-rise center was enthusiastically embraced by the Chinese. Subsequently, the thirty-eight-story China International Trade Center by Sober/Roth Design and Von Gerkan, Marg und Partner's twin nine-story German School, both in Beijing, were two pivotal tower designs brought to China by Western architects.

Slowly, and continually, more Western architects were invited into China, where the government had now set up a competition format to regulate design solicitations. In cities such as Shanghai and Shenzhen, projects of more than 3000 square meters were required to select designers using these competition programs. Throughout the 1990s, the major push for tall and super-tall buildings remained in the commercial centers of Hong Kong and Shanghai. Tall buildings arose in Beijing, the nation's capital, precipitating further debate over Western architecture and the problem of "national form."

Super-tall towers in Asia generally began to come of age in the 1980s. Prior to the first among this new generation of skyscrapers, namely Foster's 1986 Bank of Shanghai and Hong Kong, the fifty-two-story Connaught Center (now Jardine House) of 1973, and the fifty-two-story twin tower Exchange Square, built in 1985, were the tallest buildings in Hong Kong. Both projects were designed by Palmer & Turner, a longstanding British firm that had built commercial landmarks in Shanghai's Bund and Hong Kong's Central area in the early twentieth century.

In 1990, the seventy-story, 1205-foot-tall Bank of China Tower, designed by Pei Cobb Freed & Partners, initiated a trend throughout Hong Kong and Asia toward competition for the world's tallest building. Fig. 5.9 The Bank of China was controlled by the People's Republic and, in addition to manifesting characteristic political and corporate hubris, the building was a reminder by the Chinese government that, in 1997, it would regain sovereignty over Hong Kong. Since its formal opening in 1990, ten skyscrapers have exceeded the Bank of China in height, and more are on the way.

Similarly, Skidmore Owings & Merrill's Jin Mao Tower in Shanghai has brought worldwide attention to both mainland China and Shanghai since opening in 1998. Fig. 5.11 Underscoring Pudong's presence as an

international financial capital, the eighty-eight-story tower comprises 3 million square feet of space, including a retail galleria at its base and an atrium-style Grand Hyatt hotel atop multiple floors of Class A office space. A highly visible symbol of China's evolution from purely traditional architecture, or, in the case of Shanghai, European neoclassical architecture, the tower represents a kind of global modernism inflected with Chinese ornament. In China, this race toward the super-tall building began in highly commercialized cities such as Shanghai and Shenzhen, and spread later to the country's government center of Beijing. High-rise architects who had by now worked in China for more than a decade continued to build super-tall buildings into the new millennium, such as KPF's Plaza 66 in 2002 and John Portman's sixty-story Tomorrow Square of 2004. All of the new towers were being designed by American firms at a time when the U.S. was experiencing a serious economic downturn in its own commercial real estate activity. Being brought in to deliver Western architectural icons and standards of service, these firms found major new profit centers outside their flagging economies.

In November 2001, China entered the World Trade Organization (WTO) after years of intense lobbying. Shanghai continues today to build urgently and looks to its sponsorship of the 2010 World Exposition, much as Beijing readied itself for the 2008 Olympic Games. Massive construction blankets cities attempting to signify, through architecture, their new participation in the world order. While Beijing ramped up to receive a million and a half visitors to the Games, global television coverage was the real game here. The city added 4,000 high-end hotel rooms in 2007 alone, and an additional 7,000 for the following year. The Mandarin Oriental is expanding, among a deluge of other luxury chains, just as the smaller boutique hotel circuit, begun in America, is spreading throughout China. Celebrated architects Zhu Pei, Kengo Kuma and Steven Holl have designed small unique hotels in Beijing. Fig. 5.10 While most of the extraordinary works of architecture are cultural and recreational buildings, residential towers and vertical hotels are opening as well as iconic business buildings such as OMA's CCTV. Fig. 5.12 Seldom in the modern period, has a culture created an opportunity for architectural experimentation at such a grand scale.

Beyond China, Kuala Lumpur's eighty-eight-story Petronas Towers opened in 1998 as the world's tallest building and as iconic twin towers. Initiated by the prime minister of Malaysia, the project, in addition to constituting a major advertisement for the state oil company, was intended to draw world attention to this Southeast Asian country. Ironically, one year before its opening, international investments took flight and its currency collapsed. In 2004, Taipei, the capital city of Taiwan, aiming to draw attention to its economic and cultural successes, created the 101-story Taipei 101, the world's most recent tallest building. Located in the Xin-Yi District, Taipei 101, which is visible on the skyline for many miles, was the largest engineering project in Taiwan. A state-of-the-art commercial office building for multinational merchants, the tower is equipped with the latest communication infrastructure comprised of fiber optics, microwave and satellite backups. Advanced information security systems have been installed to prevent hacking or information leakage from its broadband network. The skyscraper's two observatory shuttle elevators are the fastest in the world, traveling upward at 3300 feet per minute.

The Middle East

Until the early 1970s, many of the high-rise buildings in European capital cities were hotels designed and built for American hotel companies. Similarly, yet with less frequency, Western hotels began to appear in the Middle East, such as the fourteen-story Istanbul Hilton designed by SOM's Gordon Bunshaft in 1955. The Hilton Tel Aviv opened in 1965, followed by the twenty-one-story Jerusalem Hilton. CP Hotels then entered the region, as did InterContinental, Holiday Inn and Sheraton. Although generally undistinguished for their architecture, these hotels were modern efficient tall buildings. Modernism in the region consequently became associated with a kind of amenity-rich internationalism. Israel's Jerusalem and Tel Aviv, Egypt's Cairo, and select locations within the Kingdom of Saudi Arabia experienced the construction of tall buildings in this period. These Middle Eastern countries, which had maintained ongoing political and commercial relations with both Europe and the United States, tended to import the Western high-rise building type and like Asia, the Western designers who produced them.

In a country of few tall buildings, a unique and profoundly important skyscraper in its day was the 1983 National Commerce Bank in Jeddah, Saudi Arabia designed by Gordon Bunshaft. Fig. 5.14 Iconic and Western in its pure triangular form, the building represented a clear environmental response to the desert's harsh heat and light. Fully clad with opaque stone, each exterior tower elevation was punched with a giant rectangular opening that admitted natural light, shade

and ventilating air into a central atrium within the core of the building. In pursuit of environmentally thoughtful strategies, many skyscrapers since (Norman Foster's Commerzbank, notably among them) have incorporated the lessons of this building into their own.

Thanks to mounting oil revenues, the commercialization that followed, and an openness to Western culture, places like Riyadh in Saudi Arabia, Doha in Qatar, and Dubai, Abu Dhabi and Bahrain in the United Arab Emirates, have initiated a recent history of commercial office buildings, hotels and now, residential towers that house significant portions of their royal and middle class families, as well as the swelling ranks of business expatriates. Fig. 5.15 – Fig. 5.19

Until fifty years ago, when oil was discovered, Dubai and similar settlements on the Persian Gulf were small Bedouin fishing villages, identified with pearl diving and shipping. As recently as twenty years ago, there was little to place these emirates on the world map. Through a highly publicized strategy of economic diversification, the liberalization of business protocols, and the construction of a regional re-export capability, Dubai has managed to establish itself as an international logistics, financial, retail and recreational center, referring to itself as the "Singapore of the Middle East." With oil reserves estimated to run out within a decade, Dubai has directed its sixteen percent annual growth into non-oil related venues and boasts that fifty percent of its gross domestic product is service-based. As a result of this precipitous growth, guest workers make up some ninety percent of the population and ninety-nine percent of its private workforce.

In an attempt to set themselves apart and control their immediate surroundings, some of the most recent high-rise projects have relocated outside Dubai's old town, Burj Dubai. Virtually no tall buildings existed there prior to the late 1990s, and the first to gain worldwide attention was the fifty-two-story Burj Al Arab, Fig. 5.16 an exotic sail-shaped glass-and-concrete tower, designed by Atkins and sited offshore on a manmade island. Completed in 1999, the skyscraper is triangular in plan with hotel suites lining two sides of a 182-meter-tall atrium. A year later, the twin Jumeirah Emirates Towers, designed by Hazel Wong of the NORR Group, opened as a fully integrated mixed-use commercial center. Fig. 5.18 Distant from the historic core and nearby services, the project internalizes many functions with wrap-around parking for 1,800 cars, a two-story indoor retail and restaurant street, plus two fifty-two-story towers, one for office and the other for hotel. Triangular in plan, not unlike the Burj Al Arab, the buildings are wrapped in glass and silver gray metal with two rooflines sloping toward each other. Among the many recent and repetitive towers which line Sheikh Zayed Road, Dubai's principal commercial strip, the towers have been widely recognized as the first modern icons of this business-friendly state's new vertical culture.

Although many elaborate skyscraper projects are now both in design and under construction in Dubai, none has captured the world's attention nor appeared to be such a pressing symbol of the state's arrival at the world stage as the $800 million Burj Dubai, slated to be the tallest building in the word when completed, in 2009. Fig. 5.19 Designed by the Chicago office of SOM, the actual height of the building is being kept secret to suppress competition. If the estimated height of 2,300 feet proves true, the tower will surpass the world's current tallest building, Taiwan's Taipei 101, at 1,700 feet. Burj Dubai is a three-pronged tower in plan with round-ed vertical shafts that drop off in spiraling fashion as the tower ascends. Braced in this way against lateral wind forces, the larger bottom floors will house a hotel designed by Giorgio Armani, above which will be located 1000 apartments. Restaurants, pools, fitness centers and lounges will be located in the mid-section, with the smaller top floors dedicated to offices.

Prior to commencing the project, the Dubai-based developer Emaar Properties, an entity that is linked to the prime minister and whose chief executive officer is also the director general of the Department of Economic Development, reviewed the success of Kuala Lumpur City Centre. Not only were the Petronas Towers an important part of that project's identity, but the addi-tion of a major shopping center, a large-scale artificial lake and park, and a hotel allowed the project to be both large enough and diverse enough to shift the center of the city in its direction. Acknowledging the impor-tance of additional mixed-use elements, RNL, the master planner for the Malaysian project, was retained to plan the remainder of the Burj Dubai, using a similar model.

In its attempt to capture more international business and financial trade, and establish itself as the export capital for the region, the Dubai government is now planning Dubai World Center, a mixed-use commercial new town, for a site twenty-five miles south of Dubai's evolving central city. Planned around the new international airport, the huge, multi-phased development will extend over an area of fifty-four square miles. The heart of the new metropolis will be called Commercial City and will ultimately include up to 850 tall buildings. Like various econom-ic zones in China, which predict similar levels of growth and density, one can imagine the skyscraper here in a reverse figure/ground relationship to the city from that of the Western skyscraper. No longer an isolated icon, these skyscrapers may ultimately be viewed as infill buildings shoulder to shoulder within a uniform fabric of tall buildings.

Russia

As the price of energy worldwide rises, so does the economy of Russia, which controls significant reserves of oil and natural gas. After the break-up of the Soviet Union, Russia saw an influx of refugees into the capital city of Moscow plus a high rate of unemployment and supply shortages. In 1990, city officials began to plan a major business center outside the heart of the city analogous to Paris' La Défense and London's Canary Wharf with, at the time, little viability and no investment. By the end of the 1990s, the economy had stabilized, Russia was enjoying high revenues and the international business community was looking to partici-pate in its markets.

Moskva-City, otherwise known as the Moscow International Business Center, is under construction 2½ miles from the Kremlin. Fig. 5.20 The dense, high-rise satel-lite city is estimated to cost $10 billion and is planned to provide 30 million square feet of modern business and support services on 148 acres on the Krasnopresnenskaya banks of the Moscow River. City planners assert that the expanding demand for office space was beginning to drive out housing and support services in central Moscow and the creation of Moskva-City will help to preserve the character of the historic center. In a show of support for the project, the Moscow city government is planning to relocate its offices to the site.

A mixture of uses is planned for the new satellite city, with sixty percent dedicated to office, ten percent to residential, and twenty percent retail, services and entertainment functions. An aquatic park with an indoor year-round beach will be built as a recreation-al centerpiece. The site will be dominated by the 2008-foot-tall Russia Tower, planned to be one of the world's tallest buildings and scheduled for completion in 2012. Most of the additional twenty-five high-rise buildings are projected to be open by 2010. The adjacent Moscow River will be a primary transportation route as well as a natural amenity. Direct rail lines will link the center with two of Moscow's airports and an eventual third. Ticketing, baggage check-in, customs and transportation will be provided from the center directly to the airport.[3]

The city government has subdivided the Moskva-City master plan into twenty plots that are developable by Russian and foreign investors. Among the buildings underway is a sixty-seven-story tower, designed by Swanke Hayden Connell Architects, comprised of 2 million square feet of "Class A" office space plus apartments. Nearby, NBBJ has designed a staggered twin tower plus podium scheme comprised of office, apartments, shopping mall, fitness center, swimming pool and spa. These towers will reach seventy-three and sixty-two stories.

While these efforts are being made outside the historic city, Norman Foster is proposing Moscow City Tower, the tallest building in Europe, in the heart of historic Moscow. The tower draws on earlier Foster work from his Tokyo Millennium Tower of 1989 in its profile and section. Its triangular plan and sky gardens recall Frankfurt's Commerzbank while its exoskeletal bracing recalls the diagrid of his Hearst Building in New York City. A sleek sloping form, the mass and height of the project have raised controversy worldwide about the appropriateness of buildings of such monolithic scale within the traditional and intimately scaled city.

Similarly, in St. Petersburg, a proposal for Gazprom City has been made on a historic site on the Neva River opposite the baroque, blue-and-white Smolny Cathedral. Fig. 5.22 The project is sponsored by Gazprom, the state-controlled energy company and the fourth largest company in the world with a capitalization of $250 billion dollars. The fact that the proposed building will be three- to four-times taller than the eighteenth century city's most famous landmark has drawn widespread protests throughout the city. Existing zoning laws forbid anything taller than forty-eight meters in this district. however, as an arm of the Kremlin, Gazprom is capable of overturning such restrictions. The British architecture firm RMJM was selected in a widely promoted competition including Jean Nouvel, Massimiliano Fuksas, Herzog and de Meuron, Rem Koolhaas and Daniel Libeskind. Nikolai Tanayev, general director of Gazprom Neft Invest, the subsidiary overseeing the project, has responded to criticism by likening its development to the construction of Paris' Eiffel Tower.[4]

In 1996, eight of the world's ten tallest buildings were in the U.S., and all except Chicago's John Hancock Center were office towers. The remaining two were Hong Kong's tallest office towers, Central Plaza and Bank of China. By the year 2010, it is expected that all ten of the world's tallest buildings will be in developing nations, and most of these will be mixed-use skyscrapers.

FutureTall is the future of super-tall. Today's Western skyscraper is nowhere the ultimate symbol of aspiration as it is in developing countries in Asia and the Middle East. Many questions are being asked, from the architectural ones which may be the least of these, to the economic and social ones. With such a persistent need to distinguish each tower through form, details, materials, and amenities, can these and other choices inherent in the design process become extrinsic and irrelevant to the potential for crafting and advancing the skyscraper typology? Can these choices, in the context of national ambitions and commercial showmanship, be anything more than signifiers of a new luxury product category? Is the future of super-tall buildings simply a retail phenomenon at a new and vastly larger scale? On the economic and social fronts, what is the true expense of these buildings frequently built in the capitals of energy production and consumption, considering the presently incalculable costs of resourcing, manufacturing and erecting them? And who, over what time frame, pays for these costs? A real interest in asking these questions is growing as are our efforts in finding tools to measure the answers. All this will inform the critique of a next generation of FutureTall.

Notes

[1] Greco, Joann, *Building a New Tokyo*, Urban Land, July 2007, op. cit., 72.

[2] Chen, Aric, *The Road to Beijing*, The New York Times, August 19, 2007, Travel, op. cit., 1.

[3] Holley, David, *Amid Oil Boom, A New Moscow Rises*, Los Angeles Times, July 31, 2007, op. cit., A5.

[4] Myers, Steven Lee, *Russian Window on the West Reaches for the Sky*, The New York Times, International, November 28, 2006, op. cit. A4.

Fig. 5.1 Roppongi Hills, Tokyo, 2003. Mori Building Co., Ltd.;
Kohn Pedersen Fox Associates, The Jerde Partnership, Fumihiko
Maki, Terence Conran.

Fig. 5.2 Top floor, Mori Tower at Roppongi Hills.
Kohn Pedersen Fox Associates.

Fig. 5.3 Shinju-ku, Tokyo, 1986. Thomas Struth, photographer.

Fig. 5.4 Tokyo Midtown, Tokyo, 2006. Skidmore, Owings & Merrill.

Fig. 5.5 Plaza, Tokyo Midtown. Skidmore, Owings & Merrill.

Fig. 5.6 Hong Kong, 2005.

Fig. 5.7 Great Wall Hotel, Beijing, 1983. Ellerbe Becket.

Fig. 5.8 Shanghai Center, Shanghai, 1989.
John Portman & Associates.

Fig. 5.9 Bank of China, Hong Kong, 1990.
Pei Cobb Freed & Partners.

Fig. 5.10 Linked Hybrid model, Beijing, 2008.
Steven Holl Architects.

Fig. 5.11 Jin Mao Tower, Shanghai, 1998.
Skidmore, Owings & Merrill.

Fig. 5.12 Central Chinese Television Headquarters (CCTV) rendering, Beijing, 2008. Rem Koolhaas/Office for Metropolitan Architecture.

Fig. 5.13 Phare Tower rendering, La Défense, Paris, 2008.
Thom Mayne/Morphosis.

198

Fig. 5.14 National Commercial Bank, Jeddah, 1983.
Gordon Bunshaft/Skidmore, Owings & Merrill.

Fig. 5.15 Kingdom Centre, Riyadh, 2002. Ellerbe Becket and Omrania & Associates.

Fig. 5.16 Burj Al Arab, Dubai, 1999. Atkins.

Fig. 5.17 Doha High-Rise Office Building, Doha, 2008. Ateliers Jean Nouvel.

Fig. 5.18 Jumeirah Emirates Towers, Dubai, 2000.
NORR Group Consultants International and Hazel WS Wong.

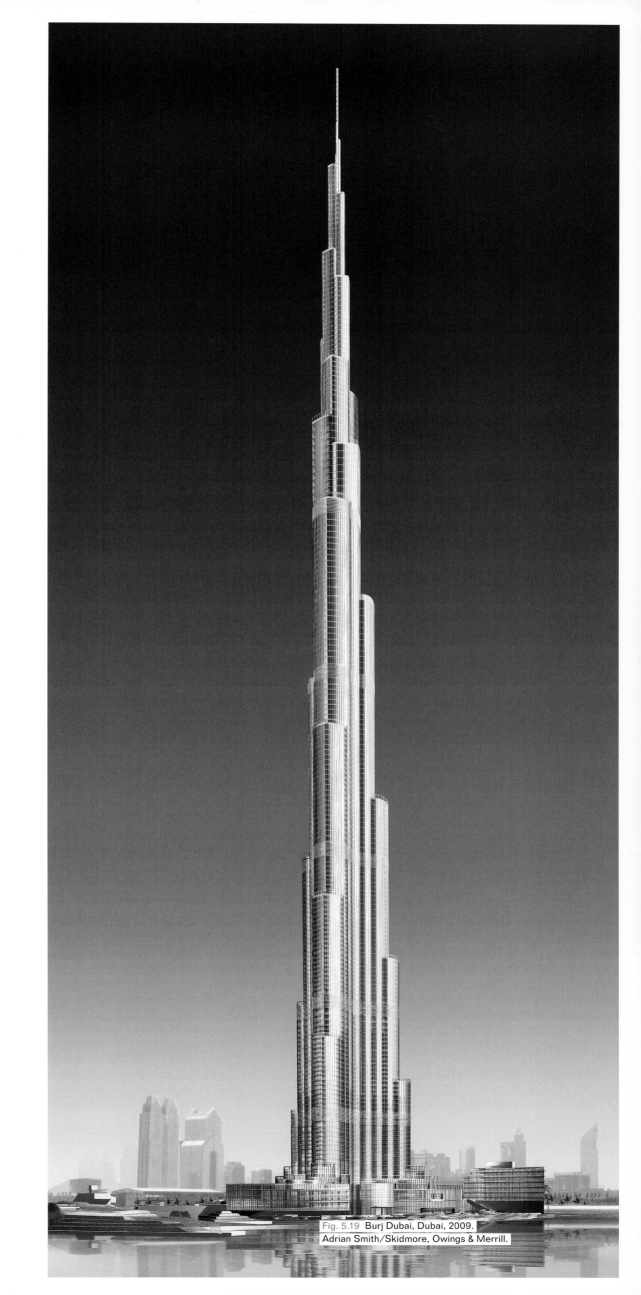

Fig. 5.19 Burj Dubai, Dubai, 2009.
Adrian Smith/Skidmore, Owings & Merrill.

Fig. 5.20 Moskva-City rendering, Moscow, 2008. Gennady Sirota.

Fig. 5.21 Moscow City Tower rendering, Moscow, 2008.
Foster + Partners.

Fig. 5.23 Fiera Milano Redevelopment, rendering of three
office towers, Milan, 2004. Left: Studio Daniel Libeskind;
middle: Arata Isozaki; right: Zaha Hadid.

Fig. 5.24 Groningen Forum, rendering, Groningen, 2006.
UNStudio.

Chapter 6

Art Skyscrapers

FutureTall
Designer
Skyscraper
The Environmental
Skyscraper
The Enrichment
of Vertical Space
Inevitable
Skyscraper

Art Skyscrapers

While certain architectures over time have been considered "artistic" or "artful," the idea of modern art's ambiguous and ambient relationship to modern architecture is one that continues to provoke questions. Whether modern art and architecture are joined by the objectification of all things flowing from the dominant industrialization is an open question. Whether a union of natural sciences and an interior world of post-Freudian psychoanalysis has made fertile new kinds of abstraction and spiritualism remains another open question. What seems clear, however, is that at some point in the early twentieth century the output of both artists and architects moved into a radically new realm in which, whatever practical tasks they set out for themselves, they began to privilege conceptual thought, abstraction and a democratically enabled social critique. The many paths from there to here nearly a century later have been variously chronicled and constitute the platform upon which we will now consider the tall building as art. Our interest here is in the admittedly ambiguous interplay between activities in the worlds of fine arts and architecture in the recent period, with a particular focus on implications for the skyscraper form. Some connections are explicit while others are, or could be, only suggestive. In this regard, surely we have observed the work of architects whose production is impervious to the bearings of fine art; this would likely apply to the majority of building production. We are familiar with the work of architects who appear to be influenced by the artistic zeitgeist within which they operate, but fail to acknowledge any direct connection to it. In these pages, Ludwig Hilberseimer comes to mind. Then, we know the work of polymaths who move fluidly between the worlds of both art and architecture and, with some care, we can identify the elements of an overall aesthetic system from which their works are drawn. Le Corbusier was one such artist/architect. And frequently due to their own considerable commentary, we know the projects of highly reflective architects who attempt to place their work within the concerns of what we think of as art. Peter Eisenman has been a standout here. Finally, there are many studio, conceptual and performance artists who recall the concerns or primary structures of architecture in their artmaking. Donald Judd, James Turrell, and Robert Wilson are among the many.

All these conditions appear relevant to informing a broad-based commentary on the skyscraper. Artists and architects, however defined, look to each other for connection, stimulation and validation. It is in this exchange that the idea and the image of the skyscraper form may become most distilled.

Minimalism Three Times

While early modernism and what might be called "minimalism" in either art or architecture are by no means identical, minimalist works appear to be one of the various outcomes of the broader cultural phenomenon identified as modernism. One of the central prospects for a new modernism at the turn of the twentieth century was that it could be transcultural and transhistorical, evolving out of a nineteenth century that had been known for its nationalist industries, wars and cultural production. In painting, the English critics Clive Bell and Roger Fry described the key element of the new century's art as form — "significant form" and "expressive form," respectively. Escaping the weight of associational nationalism, history and academic traditions, many thought that form in works of art, similar to the element of sound in music, could independently evoke responses from the observer irrespective of any specific content involved. Considerations of such an abstract art, purified of any narrative, set the stage for work such as Kazimir Malevich's *Black Square*, exhibited in St. Petersburg in December 1915. Fig. 6.1 Early encounters with cubism, and its formal reconstruction

of the traditionally representational physical realm, gave way to works by Russian suprematists such as Malevich, and Europeans including Mondrian, Reitveld and van Doesburg, who initiated projects of pure abstraction. Rather than referencing pictorial content in their paintings and then deconstructing it as a method for exhibiting the radical and newly empowered artistic act, works like *Black Square* opened up the possibility of an entirely abstract work of art, hermetic and historic.

While the works and writings of European architects such as Le Corbusier, Hilberseimer and Mies van der Rohe were formative in the second decade, by 1922, the imagery they all embraced was sharply modernist, and one could say, in part, minimalist. The glass monoliths Le Corbusier presented in his exhibition of *A Contemporary City for Three Million Inhabitants* appeared as minimalist sculpture in the strictest sense, repetitive rectangular prisms writ large and articulated by only the most subtle scorelines to indicate floors. This minimalist language, notwithstanding the visual complexity of the ground plane or the architecture of his various smaller commissions, continued through the 1920s. His vision began to absorb new complexities following his extended trip to South America in 1929 and his trip to New York in the early '30s. By the time of his Algiers tower and his several Unité projects, his understanding of building technologies and his aspirations for the architectonic detail of his work had become enriched. While his early status as a theoretician appears to have allowed him to conjure up an entire city made up of minimalist building objects, the more prolific and diverse building production of his later years led him to internalize many of the complexities of the city within a single building commission. For Le Corbusier, the minimal and polemically succinct building object eventually gave way to a more fully formed and expressive architectural language.

In Germany, Ludwig Hilberseimer's elaboration of the tall building form was focused both on the notions of organizing and neutralizing the flow of monolithic institutional capital in the building of the city and the meticulous ordering of height and bulk, land use, circulation, and exposure to light and air. Notwithstanding his theoretically complex approach to issues, his 1924 drawings, Project for a High-Rise City, embody a monumentally static and minimalist representation of buildings and circulation systems as objects: wide planes, horizontally layered slabs, and vast blocks fenestrated with a repetitive pattern of black squares.

Ludwig Mies van der Rohe was perhaps less concerned about the city as a whole and envisioned a building as a prospect for symbolic transformation of the city from within. Many of his early drawings present austere, reductive images scraped clean of ornament or semiotic detail of any kind. To fully understand his conception for the glass skyscraper proposals of 1922, one must acknowledge certain connections to German Expressionism as delivered by Bruno Taut, Hans Poelzig and Hermann Finsterlin. Nevertheless, his charcoal and graphite elevation drawings are minimalist in the extreme.

While modernism took off in all directions following the experiments of the early 1920s, a persistent strain of minimalism survived the next four decades as a number of young architects had matured and were now working internationally. America began to embrace this new aesthetic strain, marrying it to its own newfound prominence in world affairs and commerce. It could be said that, by this time, no one had more authority to revive interest in this minimalist strain than Mies van der Rohe, as displayed in his campus design for Chicago's Illinois Institute of Technology (1939) Fig. 6.4 and New York's Seagram Building (1958). Charles Jencks' amusing 1977 comparison of the IIT boiler house and chapel in which Jencks claimed to be unable to discern any appreciable difference between the two, could have perfectly described the semiotic silence of minimalist art that was rearing its head again at not so coincidentally the same time as minimalist architecture.[1] Throughout the 1950s and '60s, the exceptional work of international architects like Skidmore, Owings & Merrill, Arne Jacobsen, Gio Ponti and Hentrich-Petschnigg was overtaken in numbers by lesser corporate firms as the growing taste for minimalist form converged with the expeditious delivery of leasable commercial office space. Minimalist monoliths provided swift urban infill for many American cities and European capitals for years to come.

The cover of the March 1967 issue of *Arts Magazine* read "A Minimal Future? Art as Object 1958-1968." The decade in question was the same decade which followed the opening of the Seagram Building and the proliferation of minimalist skyscrapers. Fig. 6.7 In the world of fine arts, the movement was now being legitimized, its polemics dissected, its members identified and its future debated. As Ann Goldstein has written in a Museum of Contemporary Art exhibition of the same name, "Art's associative or symbolic function was being renegotiated in favor of its conception as a self-referential object."[2] She went on to say that these so-called minimalists represented "a range of distinct and heterogeneous, yet related, strategies. In fact, between 1958 and 1968 many

minimalisms challenged prevailing aesthetic forms and served to propel a redefinition of the 'object status' of a work of art into conceptual terms as they redefined the structure, form, material, and production of the art object, as well as its relationship to space."[3] The historic roots of the movement have been variously debated, but many have cited the earlier generation of Russian constructivists and suprematists, Tatlin, Rodchenko, Vesnin and Malevich as the movement's aesthetic forebears. In its own time, the work is often considered a reaction to the many modern abstract and abstract expressionist schools of art, all of which questioned the presumptive authority of traditional European artworks.

The cover of this seminal *Arts Magazine* issue featured Buckminster Fuller's photo-collage of a giant pyramidal city floating in the New York City harbor. Fig. 6.6 In the magazine, the artist Dan Graham reviewed three recent New York exhibitions: Scale Models and Drawings at the Dwan Gallery, Architectural Sculpture, Sculpture Architecture at the Visual Arts Gallery, and Macrostructures at the Richard Feigen Gallery. Graham described both the utopian and fantasy architectural works of monumental scale, as well as the smaller sculptural works that "subvert notions of the monumental, the architectural" within the scale of the gallery.

In another article, the critic Jean Perreault cited a 1966 exhibition entitled Primary Structures, presented at the Jewish Museum, which included the work of forty-two sculptors from New York and Great Britain. In an early acknowledgement of the cross-fertilization of art practices, the curator Kynaston McShine wrote, "Increasingly in recent years, both the artist and his audience reject rigid categories, or the traditional limits of media. It is tradition that makes us arbitrarily fix boundaries and esthetic categories. Depending upon the way in which space is used and occupied by a form, the material means and the artist's intention, as we may understand it, we name the work a 'painting' or a 'sculpture.'"[4] He might have gone on to say "or architecture." In fact, a certain portion of the very best skyscraper designs in this period, and for some time thereafter, could well have been described by McShine's final reference to the minimalist artwork: "These structures are conceived as 'objects,' abstract, directly experienced, highly simplified and self-contained. There is no overt surrealistic content in the sculpture, and the anthropomorphic is rejected. The structures are generally not 'compositions.' Shape, color and material have a physical concreteness and unity that is both elegant and monumental, expressive or restrained, but always challenging."[5]

Much has been written about the reactionary movements in the arts and architecture that followed. In architecture, a general consensus formed around the term postmodernism, which rejected both the modernist belief in progress and the prevalence of reason, as well as the many impoverished architectural monoliths that appeared to celebrate technology in lieu of human culture and social context. Jump-started from a range of sources including Jane Jacobs' *Death and Life of Great American Cities* (1961) and Robert Venturi's *Complexity and Contradiction in Architecture* (1966), Charles Jencks catalogued and canonized the movement in 1977 with *The Language of Post-Modern Architecture.* It took on many forms but drew its initial focus by seeing architecture as a form of linguistics, a semiotic system wherein elements of architecture became signifiers of meaning. From this perspective, classic modern architecture was presumed to have failed grandly, as it was perceived to be technocratic, object-like and non-communicative. For a moment, practitioners as diverse as Robert Stern, Aldo Rossi, Peter Eisenman and Kisho Kurokawa all came in under the new postmodern tent.

Before long, criticisms of pseudo-profundity, elitist references to remote historical events, and the popularization of classical architectural motifs began to flood the intellectual marketplace. Impressed with the dense jargon of an assortment of mostly French linguists and philosophers, and with the support of a 1988 Museum of Modern Art exhibition of the same name, deconstructivism took aim at the waning postmodern styles. This cultural nano-event however was short-lived as purportedly deconstructivist architects failed to translate intellectual constructs into meaningful architectural ones. As Hans Ibelings has reported, "Here Derrida's philosophy of deconstruction was converted into a pseudo-chaos of oblique angles, and Deleuze's metaphor of the fold was translated into folded floors and walls."[6] Although, deconstructivism was introduced as a break with postmodernism, "like postmodernism, deconstructivism rests on the pillar of symbolic meaning whereby architectural form is seen as metaphorical."[7]

By the 1990s an interest in the canon of modern architecture reappeared. While much had changed during the intervening style wars, a new generation of architects had matured, new materials and technologies were advancing, and an attention to the use of energy and sustainability topped architects' list of priorities. Building programs were now denser, often conflicted and hybrid, and the city was a more complex place in which to build, creating an attractive stage for the sentimental return of the iconic modern form. In this new age, however, the geometric purity of the modern movement, its characteristic lack of interest in physical context and scale, and its communicative neutrality became hallmarks of its reinvention into something recently termed the "supermodern."

An extraordinary cluster of books bearing upon this reinvention suddenly appeared in the mid-1990s. Marc Augé's *Non-Places, Introduction to an Anthropology of Supermodernity* (1995) served as the philosophical guidebook through the new territory. Terence Riley's Museum of Modern Art exhibition catalogue, Light Construction (1995), captured architecture that exhibited new attention to surfaces in the age of electronic media and informed by the intricacies of visual perception. This work dovetailed nicely with Daniela Colafranceschi's book of the same year, *Architettura in Superficie; Materiali, Figure e Tecnologie della Nuove Facciate Urbane,* exploring the emergence of smooth, translucent and transparent building facades. Fig. 6.8 Finally, two important books were published with interrelated themes: Rodolfo Machado and Rodolphe el-Khoury's 1995 *Monolithic Architecture* and Vittorio Savi and Josep M. Montaner's 1996 *Less is More, Minimalism in Architecture and the Other Arts.* The confluence of these writings documented the arrival of a new set of conditions to which architecture was responding with a new set of strategies.

Nothing sets the tone for a discussion of the supermodern like the prologue in Marc Augé's brief book. In it, he describes a human episode characterized by streaming global marketing, homogenized product lines and omnipresent capitalism, yet stripped of personal contact and geographic context. Augé's protagonist sits on an airplane skimming a magazine when a book review entitled "Euromarketing" momentarily catches his attention: "The homogenization of needs and consumption patterns is one of the overall trends characterizing the new international business environment ... Starting from an examination of the effects of the globalization phenomenon on European business, on the validity and content of Euromarketing and on predictable developments in the international marketing environment, numerous issues were discussed."[8]

As Terence Riley noted in his MOMA show and catalogue, few of the celebrated projects in the show appeared to exhibit any interest in formal considerations, rather they focused on surface. Large glassy buildings were, in many cases, nothing more than a simple "rectangular volume." A kind of formal reduction, or minimalism, unites many of these projects and the work reviewed in the contemporaneous literature. The architecture of thoughtful and widely published architects including OMA, Dominique Perrault, Toyo Ito, Herzog & de Meuron, Jean Nouvel and Kazuyo Sejima appears relevant here. Fig. 6.9 The work as a whole comes together for its attention to a homogenization of surface, a kind of neutrality and an object quality, obvious in its physical context for its monopolizing scale. Hans Ibelings, in his 2002 book, *SuperModernism: Architecture in the Age of Globalization,* refers to this "sensitivity to the neutral" as the essence of the supermodern. Differentiating it from its predecessors, postmodernism and deconstructivism, and their sense of boundless space, Ibelings states, "This boundless space is no dangerous wilderness or frightening emptiness, but rather a controlled vacuum, for if there is one thing that characterizes this age it is total control."[9] He goes on to draw a connection between notions such as "undefinedness, boundlessness and neutrality" and the same issues outside of architecture which Augé references. The invisibility of globalized systems, cyberspace, telecommunications, travel and new media, appear to have redefined historic definitions of space itself. A life suffused with travel has revised the commodity of space into "a zone that is traversed, an interval in a continuous movement interrupted at most for a brief stopover."[10] This redefinition of space reminds us of Rem Koolhaas' inventory of new space, suggested by the linguistic morphing of virtual terms such as "chat rooms, Web sites and firewalls": "waning spaces once celebrated, now hemorrhaging aura; contested spaces, continuously defined by the battles for their dominion; and new spaces, only recently understood as space at all."[11] One of architecture's reactions to these shifting and chaotic taxonomies appears to be a new kind of extreme minimalism, a simultaneous expansion and contraction of sorts on the existing urban landscape. The supermodern skyscraper asserts itself with uncompromising scale even as its evermore complex inner workings become shrouded in quiescent form. Fig. 6.10

Domesticities and the Informational Tower

A surprising trend that has emerged over the past forty years among a wide range of artists concerns the public display of domesticity in all its specific detail. Recalling an earlier appropriation of domestic objects into the world of surrealism and Duchamp's "ready-mades," advocacy movements in the 1960s elevated individual action and social radicalism in various forms, focusing the attention of artists, once again, on the domestic landscape. Today this continuing

examination of the details of a life individually lived now thrust into a world of higher technologies and global exposure has made possible a union of the most intimate domestic detail with the most public forms of visual expression. Many artists and architects have explored this dialectic of the domestic artifact and its relationship to public examination writ large, frequently transforming the meaning of the large building, or skyscraper, in the process. Further developments are certain to follow.

The adaptation of a large building to human habitation seems to imply the multiplication of individual spheres of living. Implicit in the skyscraper, then, is the notion of the human module, be it a home, an apartment, an office, workstation or, in some cases, a form of specialized furniture. Familiar modernist strategies have tended toward the generalization of these elements and a search for a monolithic definition of demand met by a monolithic design solution. Many contemporary artists, however, theorize a realm of highly individualized zones, which, taken together, theoretically make up the large building. Because of their frequent disinterest in any sense of monolithic demand, however, these artists envision a version of physical design that can appear provisional, negotiated and diverse.

One of the most visible figures in this trend has been James Wines and SITE, a multidisciplinary architecture and environmental art studio based in New York City. Fig. 6.13 – Fig. 6.16 SITE's intent, over time, has been to integrate the practices of architecture, the visual arts and the surrounding physical context in a unified vision of change. Overall, the goals of the group have been to shift aesthetic evaluation in architecture away from orthodox design critiques by suggesting levels of "indeterminacy, idiosyncrasy and cultural diversity through spontaneous acts of choice, chance and change."[12] Wines has explained the underlying reasons for this approach: "The imagery that a work of architecture generates as an extension of its own functions or formal relationships is never as interesting as the ideas it can absorb from the outside." This simple idea when applied to a modernist work of architecture, or the modern skyscraper typology with its image's received and iconic meaning, can be destabilizing and subversive.

SITE's 1981 proposal for a new kind of skyscraper, Highrise of Homes, visualized a fifteen- to twenty-story concrete-and-steel frame filled with highly individual, traditional and banal images of single family homes arrayed around a central elevator and mechanical core. In this version, the familiar modern skyscraper was presented as a phantom, a silent armature designed to express the domestic ambitions of homeowners.

The semiotic power of the skyscraper and its sponsor is downplayed while the opportunity for individual statements of identity is heightened. Many drawings of this project were produced and call to mind Le Corbusier's own evolution begun with his 1934 proposal for the Viaduct Block in Algiers Fig. 6.12 through his Unité d'Habitation projects in which he appeared to acknowledge the domestic individuality of residences embedded in the larger unified building form.In more recent times, SITE's work recalls the deconstructions of Gordon Matta-Clark's "Anarchitecture," reminding one of the exhilaration and transformational meaning a tall building can convey as a vessel for artistic intervention and a view into anonymous and enigmatic contents.

A more recent SITE proposal for a tall building is the Residence Mumbai of 2004. Fig. 6.15 – Fig. 6.16 A skyscraper that advances the group's long-standing interest in vertical gardens and embraces spiritual notions of India's Vedic architecture, the tower displays SITE's characteristic interest in indeterminacy and domesticity. The tower is conceived as a vertical concrete core, which carries primary structure, vertical circulation and mechanical systems. At the top of the building is hoisted a deep cantilevered truss from which hang a number of concrete-encased steel-frame floor slabs suspended by high-strength cables. In addition to the gardens, which proliferate at multiple levels, a range of sunscreens, canopies, flex-walls and suspended ceilings are designed to adapt to each dwelling and provide a response to climate. Additional devices, such as light shelves, double-glass skins with air cavities for cooling, ventilation tubes, adjustable roof louvers, and photovoltaic panels populate the scheme, reminding us of comparable strategies in Ken Yeang's bio-climatic architecture of the Far East.

A designer who shares certain obsessions with the primordial landscape and its potentially surreal impact on the large building is the American/Argentine architect, Emilio Ambasz. Fig. 6.17 – Fig. 6.19 His intellectual interests are akin to those of SITE only to the degree that, as Michael Sorkin has referred to him, he "prefers an architecture of setting rather than orchestration." In so many other ways his vision is a unique one, as he appears to eschew theoretical deliberation and presents his work as a kind of complete paradise. His investigations into the tall building form are unparalleled and surreal. The most expressive might be his design for Nichii Obihiro Department Store in Hokkaido, Japan, from 1987. A stair-stepped jumble of hanging gardens and sheer glass planes, the proposal is a wildly expressive representation of nature and technology, clearly informing his design for

the Fukuoka Prefectural International Hall to follow in 1990. Stripped of the conceptual detail of the earlier project, and from the initial studies for the hall itself, the final building is a strange tower hybrid, a building-as-garden stair, which, in its incorporation of trays of lush planting, both climbs skyward and at the same time subverts the loftiness of a tower which has been overtaken by the verdant ground plane.

Ambasz has thoroughly investigated his version of this typology in his Worldbridge Trade and Investment Center in Baltimore as well as his Chiba Town Center in Japan, both 1989 proposals. In the first case, the building is completely overwhelmed, and subdued, by foliage, while in the second, landscape is contained within a contrasting white superframe, presented as green artifacts fastidiously isolated and showcased within the building. Finally, the most restricted variant in his ongoing search has to be the 1998 proposal for the Palace of Vertical Gardens, a redesign of the ENI Headquarters in Rome. Here, gardens are completely subsumed within the recognizable iconography of a tall building.

The convergence of post-industrial domesticity and the tall building has been evocatively detailed by much of the work of LOT-EK, the collaborative architecture studio of Ada Tolla and Giuseppe Lignano. Fig. 6.20 – Fig. 6.24 Taken from the William Gibson novel, *Johnny Mnemonic,* the name LOT-EK refers to a future-primitive tribe that lives off the scavenged detritus of the decaying city, recycling and adapting as necessary for survival. In consideration of LOT-EK's work, Philip Nobel reflects that a "pure future is a fascist future…In a democracy, new technologies don't expunge the old, they just push their rivals aside to serve the needs of other, more marginal economies. There, the old may linger, flourish, or spawn the unknowing devotions of a thousand cargo cults, but it does not die."[14] This is the physical and conceptual landscape in which LOT/EK designs. The 1996 Miller-Jones Studio comprises a steel storage container within a tall loft building and adapts it to domestic storage, kitchen, sleeping quarters and media wall. Out on the apartment's open loft floor an amalgamation of refrigerator-freezer units and Masonite door panels are cobbled together to embed storage, desktop computers and adjustable drawing boards in a centralized multi-functional work unit. The pieces are expressive and mongrel as they trade out a comprehensive and elegant vision in favor of found objects and adaptability.

LOT-EK's Mobile Dwelling Unit (MDU) emerged as a speculative design project in late 1999. The central idea was to adapt a standard forty-foot-long steel shipping container to an individual home, transportable through conventional means and installable in urban conglomerations LOT-EK refers to as "MDU Harbors." Fig. 6.20 – 6.22 The project was conceived to start with a pre-made and widely available vessel and, then, with a series of physical interventions, create unitized domestic environments of rich, yet utilitarian, variation. Completely manmade, the architects refer to the result as "artificial nature." Huge stacks of these dwelling units were theorized to create tall buildings. Applied steel frames and appended vertical stairs provide access and open space, describing a highly improvised vision of vertical living, modular yet individualized.

A continuing string of LOT-EK projects led to Mixer, the adaptation of a steel cement mixer into a futuristic media cocoon designed for lounging, viewing and dreaming. Lined inside with vertical stacks of monitors, the ice-blue interior is suffused with access to virtual reality games, movies and high-speed Internet connections. In imagining the larger spatial implications of the unit, the capsule is installable in any space, rotates radially to surveil its surroundings, and is connected along its vertical spine to power, satellite TV and other forms of interconnectivity. An even more concise and adaptable domestic unit was proposed by LOT-EK for the 2001 MOMA show *Workspheres*, which transformed an airplane cargo container into an enclosed workstation, mixing work, play, relaxation and media activities. We are easily reminded here of other self-actuated habitats from the 1960s and '70s, such as the geodesic dome home, Archigram's Cushicle and the Airstream trailer. Fig. 6.24

Andrea Zittel's A-Z ventures into the world of functionalist art represent another ongoing investigation into the deep roots from which our conventional built environments grow. Her tendencies toward order, categorization and adaptability present artful strategies that meticulously rework the connective detail we take for granted in our buildings. Fig. 6.25 – Fig. 6.27 Her projects also stand as miniaturizations and microcosms of larger issues spatially compressed into highly symbolic built artifacts.

One of Zittel's most extraordinary projects connecting detailed human activities to a comprehensive vision of vertical form is her 1993 *A-Z Body Processing Unit*. Fig. 6.25 Concealed in a black traveling case hinged in the middle, the carton opens up to reveal a vertical stack of functional trays. Noting that the kitchen and bathroom areas of a residence are functionally related, Zittel points out that they are nevertheless separated in the traditional home. In her project, intake functions are located at the top of the stack while outtake functions occupy the bottom. Featuring food storage above utensil and

plate storage, cooking and serving above cleaning, followed by drainage and recycling for human waste at the bottom, the project displays the ecology of ingestion in a starkly programmatic array of mini-floor plans constituting a unique micro-version of the human skyscraper. The high pragmatism of her proposal brings to mind the forthright mentality of Chicago's earliest skyscrapers.

Zittel's sense that modern life can be reorganized around the fusion of traditionally discrete activities and into highly visible and adaptable kits-of-parts recalls early modern projects of similar scale. We are reminded of Alexander Rodchenko's 1929 *Cupboard/ Wardrobe* for Inga as well as the later storage units of Charles and Ray Eames for Herman Miller. One of Zittel's most fully explored and experimental environments is the 2001 *A-Z Cellular Compartment Units* project. Fig. 6.26 – Fig. 6.27 Here, turning to a replicable spatial module, multiplied ten times and interconnected to accommodate a range of domestic needs, the aggregations have been viewed in museum installations as free-standing residences. Conceptually and in drawings, however, they are multiplied to represent a kind of high-rise cabinet, flexibly assembled and coded visually to express an array of functional living modules. Zittel's design displays a uniquely Western congeniality toward adaptation.

The New York-based artist, Vito Acconci, has frequently operated in the territory of building form reconceived to express the issues of art. Chiding the physical permanence of the typical skyscraper and its putative association with the potency of the male gender, Acconci produced a major sculptural work entitled *High Rise* in 1980. Fig. 6.28 Transforming the image of the tall building into a precarious and lightweight contraption of cellophane, thin wood struts, ropes and pulleys, the artist was able to inflate the structure suspended from a round and suggestive skylight above, displaying the outlines of an erect penis on the side of the newly raised structure. Skyscraper, male dominance, fragility, and the threat of collapse were stunningly fused into a singular image.

Two related Acconci projects in Santiago de Compostela, Spain, from 1996, *Park Up A Building* and *House Up A Building*, redefined the traditional borders of inside/outside and provided surprising images of a large building and the effects of rethinking its exterior walls as physical borders. Fig. 6.29 In both installations an accessible staircase was hung off the solid exterior wall of the museum, in one case exhibiting trees, benches and canopies, and in the other, elements from the home: lights, appliances, toilet and privacy walls. An ability to occupy and activate the exterior wall, which is normally conceived as a divider, brings narrative content and interactivity to it, resignifying the building/object.

The exterior surface of the tall building has become both the defining characteristic of the highly urbanized city as well as an opportunity for communication and identification in a part of the world which now merchandises information at a faster rate than product or real estate. Today, global advertising interests frequently offer fees to lease exterior wall surface in heavily trafficked neighborhoods that match or exceed those which landlords can get for the floor area behind those same walls. Architects and real estate developers struggle in certain cities to integrate continuous, yet transparent, signage into the window walls of leasable office space. New York's Times Square, London's Picadilly, Los Angeles' Sunset Strip and Tokyo's Ginza ward are all exemplary of this trend. Fig. 6.30

As artists go, Jenny Holzer has notably explored the suggestive effects of text and when applied to physical materials and structures. Her original paper posters left anonymously throughout the streets of New York City in the late '70s initiated her ongoing series known as Truisms. Short personal reflections challenging instinctive thinking and carrying broad resonance were thereafter presented in many formats: 'Protect me from what I want. Government is a burden on the people. Sloppy thinking gets worse over time. You are the one who did this to me. I experiment to see if I can stand her pain.'[13] Fig. 6.31 – Fig. 6.32

In her work these texts multiply, appear printed on paper, are dyed onto clothing, engraved into paving stones, streamed across LED panels, or projected onto billboards and buildings. Though some of the statements reflect intimate content and others are broadly political, all appear in a surprising context that stresses the interior and domestic voice of the first person. As the scale and scope of Holzer's work has increased, the tension between intimate content and the public arena transforms architectural space into narrative space.

In an important variation on the theme of adding new layers of information to large scale building is the work of Keith Sonnier, the artist best known for his work with artificial light. Following up on the original medium and incipient tectonics of Dan Flavin, Fig. 6.33 Sonnier has developed exhaustive strategies to reconstruct the images of buildings and interior environments with the intervention of artificial light strategies. Highly collaborative with architects and engineers, the artist seeks to recreate physical presence by way of source light, reflected light, color, patterning, and the architectonics of the light fixtures them-

selves and their support structures. Fig. 6.34 – Fig. 6.35 No image of a large building transformed through Sonnier's participation is better exemplified than his 1999 outdoor installation on the Kunsthaus Bregenz in Austria designed by Peter Zumthor. With the support of a specialized computer program, the exterior surfaces of the minimalist opaque glass wall were redefined nightly by alternating patterns created by the illumination of 512 red, yellow and green neon tubes. Sonnier reflects, "Light is not only energy, but can likewise be used as material, rather than just a possible way of making something else visible, even if it is not an object itself."[14]

Architects have, from the perspective of their own practices, engaged similar light strategies. Toyo Ito's 1986 Tower of the Winds in Yokohama was an attempt to utilize light and color to establish a strong pure form in the shape of a cylindrical tower. Fig. 6.36 Later, in his Sendai Mediatheque, Ito devised a more complex strategy that involved using the glass window wall to spill the contents of the building to the outside nightly, exhibiting detail, human occupation and various architectonic events within the building's transparent shell. Jean Nouvel's Agbar Tower in Barcelona (2005), static by day, becomes wildly animated by night through the intense patterning of colored lights and reflective surfaces. Many other architects from Herzog & de Meuron to SANAA have used light as a powerful modifier of physical space.

The opening quote by Doug Aitken in the catalogue to his January 2007 MOMA exhibition Sleepwalkers states: "In Sleepwalkers, the city becomes a living, breathing body merging with the diverse and constantly changing individuals who make up the city. The individuals in Sleepwalkers, in turn, move beyond their physical selves and are transformed by their surroundings. Sleepwalkers investigates the new and evolving relationships of contemporary urban life."[15] Aitken, a photographer and artist, has reconstructed the interiors of large sections of exterior wall at the museum in an attempt to convert them into giant luminous panels that convey an elaborate pictorial choreography of human activity. Aitken has chosen as his subject the private lives of five urban inhabitants who awake, address their daily routines in the city, and gradually move into more artificial and fictitious states as the nocturnal hours progress. Fig. 6.37 As these personal stories cycle, each interacts with the others' pictorial stories. While Aitken's show may be a rarified construct of museum programming, the work unleashes the prospect for a fictional personality cult of the anonymous individual and exploits the scale of the urban building to project that mythology. Like many aspects of the contemporary world

of saturated media, the prospects for
enlightenment with this advanced technology
can be exhilarating in the hands of the gifted
artist and deadening in the hands of the
average merchant.

The power of these grand surfaces, and
their potential futures, is vividly exhibited
in Aitken's *Manhattan Air Rights Project*,
a series of interpretive diagrams based upon
New York City's Department of City Planning
zoning documents. Fig. 6.38 – Fig. 6.39 Overlaid
upon pictures of existing buildings are
large shaded profiles depicting the physical
prospect of building out all of the city's
existing air rights. The opportunity presented
by these diagrams for, among other things,
the multiplication of commercial advertising
is enormous. As the value of information and
marketing content increases, the function
of streets could devolve to the sole task of
circulation and the design of tall buildings as
commercial propositions would undertake to
maximize advertising revenues. As armatures
for commercial content, tall buildings in certain
locations will find the value of their surfaces
exceeding the value of the interior space
for which they were originally conceived.
While cities like Tokyo, New York City and
Hollywood have arrived at this juncture first,
as cities continue to densify and commercial
markets globalize, others will follow. The lure
of information and the image of the skyscraper may prove to be an irresistible marriage.
And the skyscraper, already referred to
as the "enigmatic signifier,"[16] will become less
enigmatic and more signifier.

Notes

[1] Jencks, Charles, *The Language of Post-Modern Architecture*, Introduction.

[2] Goldstein, Ann, Introduction: *A Minimal Future? A Minimal Future? Art As Object 1958-1968* (MOCA), op. cit., 17.

[3] ibid., 17.

[4] ibid., 19.

[5] ibid., 19.

[6] Ibelings, Hans, *Supermodernism, Architecture in the Age of Globalization*, op. cit. 24.

[7] ibid., 24.

[8] Auge, Marc, *Non-Places, Introduction to an Anthropology of Supermodernity*, op. cit., 6.

[9] Ibelings, Hans, *Supermodernism, Architecture in the Age of Globalization*, op. cit. 62.

[10] ibid., 64.

[11] Koolhaas, Rem, *Wired*, June 2003, op. cit., 117.

[12] Wines, James, Preface, *SITE: Identity in Density*, op. cit. 8.

[13] Joselit, David, Simon, Joan & Saleci, *Renata*, Phaidon Press, Jenny Holzer, op. cit., 25.

[14] Herausgeber, Kunsthaus Bregenz, Keith Sonnier, *Public Commissions in Architecture 1990-1999*, op. cit., 128.

[15] The Museum of Modern Art, *Sleepwalkers*, Doug Aitken, op. cit., 6.

[16] Jencks, Charles, *The Iconic Building*, op. cit. 21.

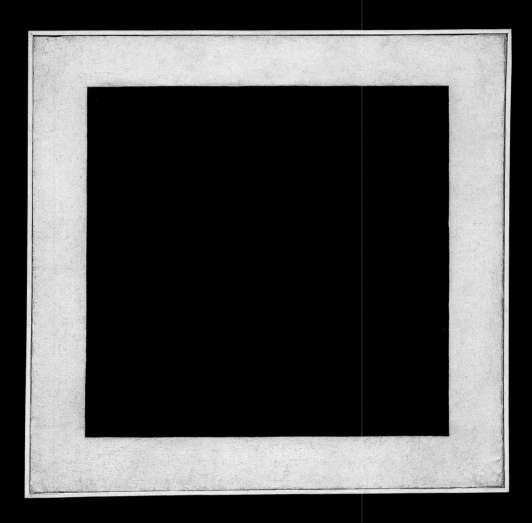

Fig. 6.1 *Black Square*, 1915. Kazimir Malevich.

Fig. 6.2 Die, 1962, fabricated 1998. Tony Smith.

Fig. 6.3 Untitled, 1965. Larry Bell.

Fig. 6.4 Photomontage of The Illinois Institute of Technology,
Chicago, 1940. Ludwig Mies van der Rohe.

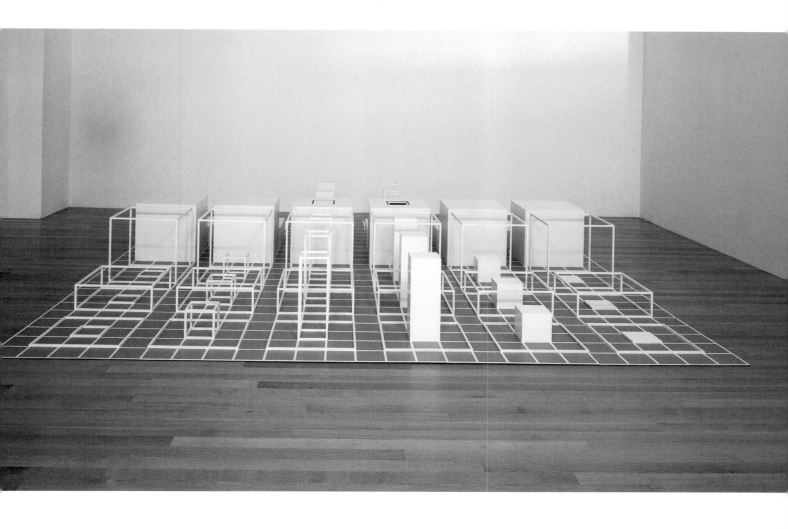

Fig. 6.5 Serial Project, I (ABCD), 1966. Sol LeWitt.

Fig. 6.6 Artwork for cover of *Arts Magazine*, New York City,
March 1967. Buckminster Fuller.

Fig. 6.7 SAS Royal Hotel, model, Copenhagen, 1960.
Arne Jacobsen.

Bregenz, 1997. Peter Zumthor.

Fig. 6.9 Bibliothéque Nationale de France, La Défense, Paris, 1996. Dominique Perrault.

Fig. 6.10 Agbar Tower, Barcelona, 2005. Ateliers Jean Nouvel.

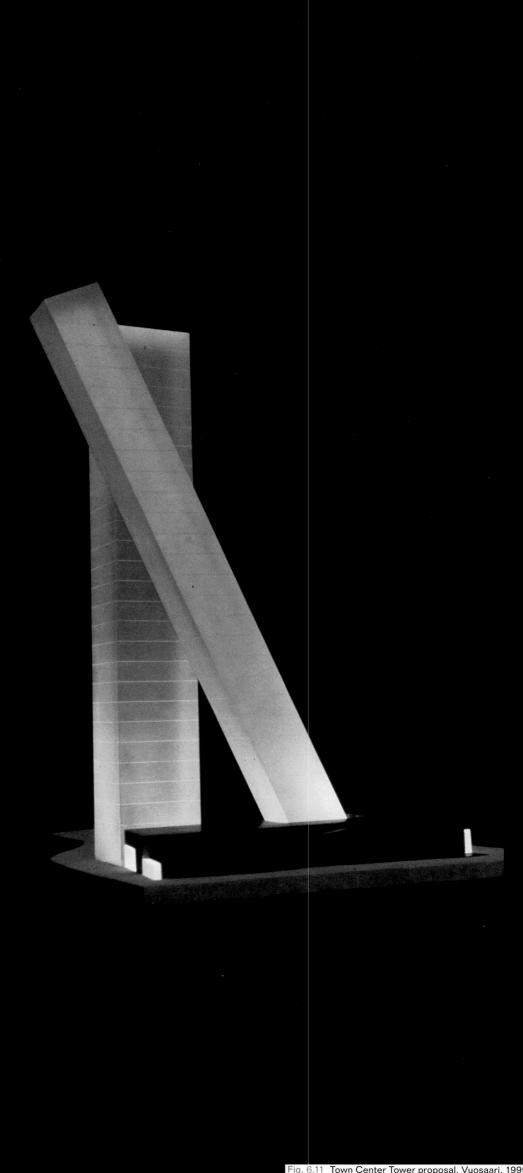

Fig. 6.11 Town Center Tower proposal, Vuosaari, 1999.
Steven Holl Architects.

Fig. 6.12 Proposal for Viaduct Block, Algiers, 1934. Le Corbusier.

Fig. 6.13 Highrise of Homes, major urban center, 1981. SITE.

Fig. 6.14 Photomontage, major urban center, 1981. SITE.

Fig. 6.15 Design proposal for Private Residential Tower,
Mumbai, 2004. SITE.

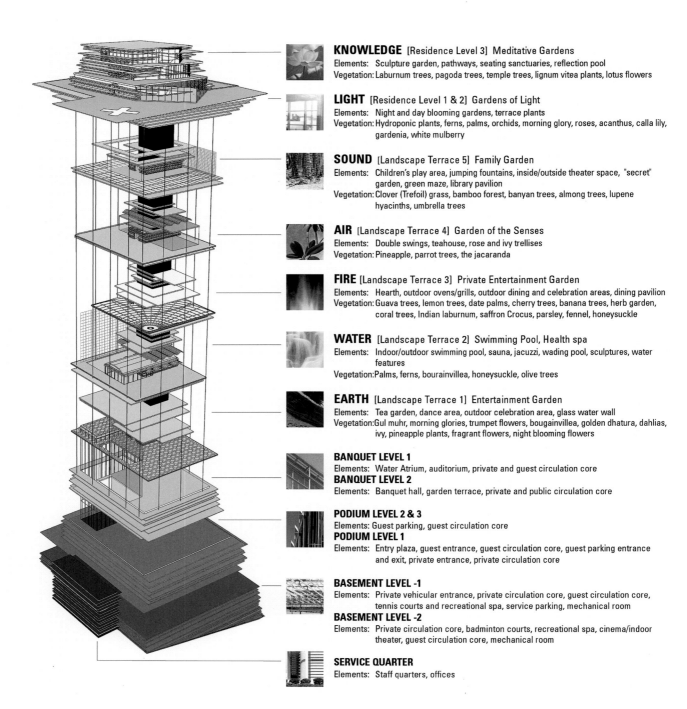

KNOWLEDGE [Residence Level 3] Meditative Gardens
Elements: Sculpture garden, pathways, seating sanctuaries, reflection pool
Vegetation: Laburnum trees, pagoda trees, temple trees, lignum vitea plants, lotus flowers

LIGHT [Residence Level 1 & 2] Gardens of Light
Elements: Night and day blooming gardens, terrace plants
Vegetation: Hydroponic plants, ferns, palms, orchids, morning glory, roses, acanthus, calla lily,
                 gardenia, white mulberry

SOUND [Landscape Terrace 5] Family Garden
Elements: Children's play area, jumping fountains, inside/outside theater space, "secret"
                 garden, green maze, library pavilion
Vegetation: Clover (Trefoil) grass, bamboo forest, banyan trees, almong trees, lupene
                 hyacinths, umbrella trees

AIR [Landscape Terrace 4] Garden of the Senses
Elements: Double swings, teahouse, rose and ivy trellises
Vegetation: Pineapple, parrot trees, the jacaranda

FIRE [Landscape Terrace 3] Private Entertainment Garden
Elements: Hearth, outdoor ovens/grills, outdoor dining and celebration areas, dining pavilion
Vegetation: Guava trees, lemon trees, date palms, cherry trees, banana trees, herb garden,
                 coral trees, Indian laburnum, saffron Crocus, parsley, fennel, honeysuckle

WATER [Landscape Terrace 2] Swimming Pool, Health spa
Elements: Indoor/outdoor swimming pool, sauna, jacuzzi, wading pool, sculptures, water
                 features
Vegetation: Palms, ferns, bourainvillea, honeysuckle, olive trees

EARTH [Landscape Terrace 1] Entertainment Garden
Elements: Tea garden, dance area, outdoor celebration area, glass water wall
Vegetation: Gul muhr, morning glories, trumpet flowers, bougainvillea, golden dhatura, dahlias,
                 ivy, pineapple plants, fragrant flowers, night blooming flowers

BANQUET LEVEL 1
Elements: Water Atrium, auditorium, private and guest circulation core
BANQUET LEVEL 2
Elements: Banquet hall, garden terrace, private and public circulation core

PODIUM LEVEL 2 & 3
Elements: Guest parking, guest circulation core
PODIUM LEVEL 1
Elements: Entry plaza, guest entrance, guest circulation core, guest parking entrance
                 and exit, private entrance, private circulation core

BASEMENT LEVEL -1
Elements: Private vehicular entrance, private circulation core, guest circulation core,
                 tennis courts and recreational spa, service parking, mechanical room
BASEMENT LEVEL -2
Elements: Private circulation core, badminton courts, recreational spa, cinema/indoor
                 theater, guest circulation core, mechanical room

SERVICE QUARTER
Elements: Staff quarters, offices

Fig. 6.16 Private Residential Tower, Axonometric – Garden
Themes and Environmental Studies. SITE.

Fig. 6.17 Nichii Obihiro Department Store proposal,
Hokkaido, 1987. Emilio Ambasz.

Fig. 6.18 Fukuoka Prefectural International Hall, Fukuoka, 1990.
Emilio Ambasz.

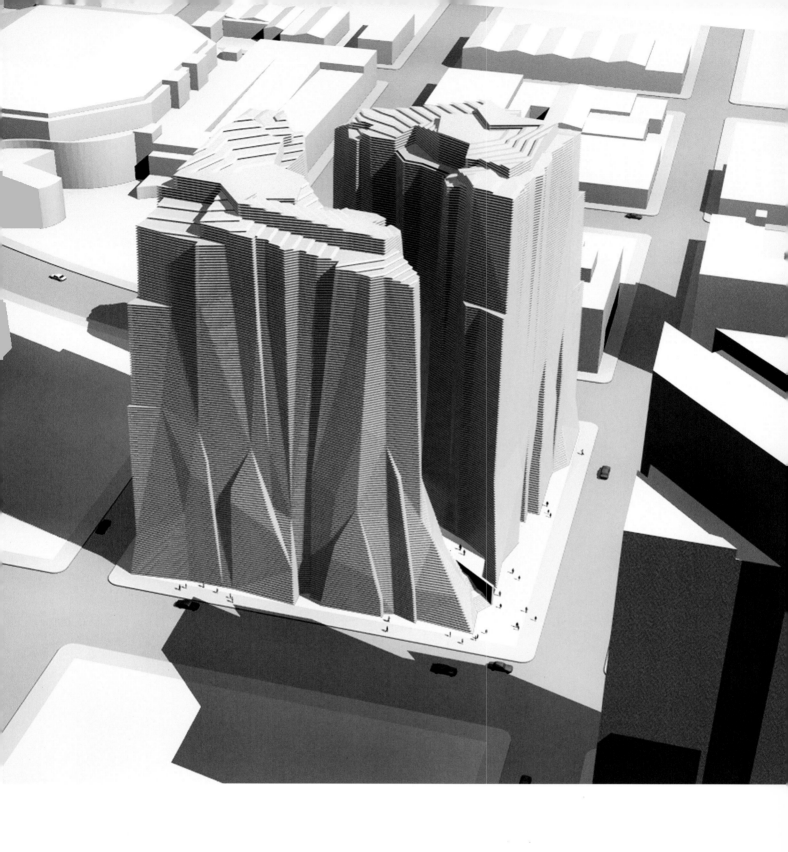

Fig. 6.19 Monument Tower Offices, Phoenix, 1998. Emilio Ambasz.

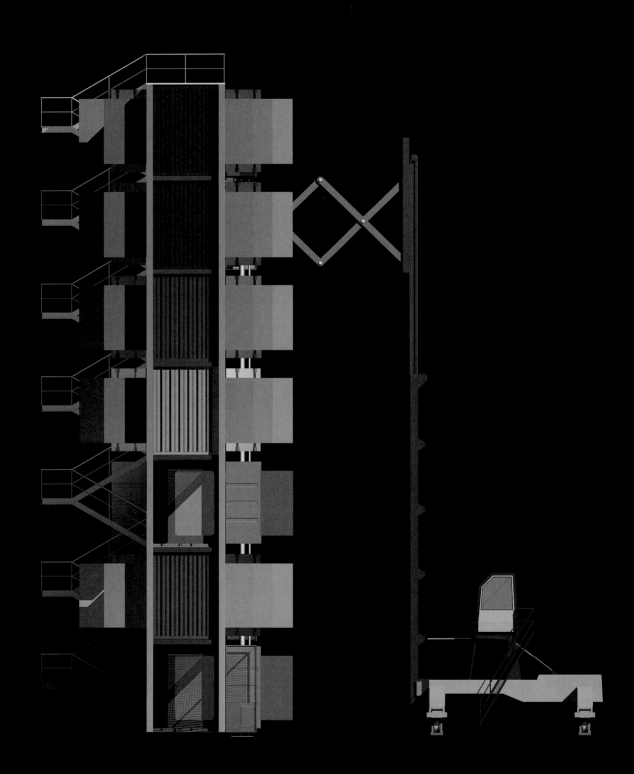

Fig. 6.20 MDU (Mobile Dwelling Unit), 1999. LOT-EK.

Fig. 6.21 MDU. LOT-EK.

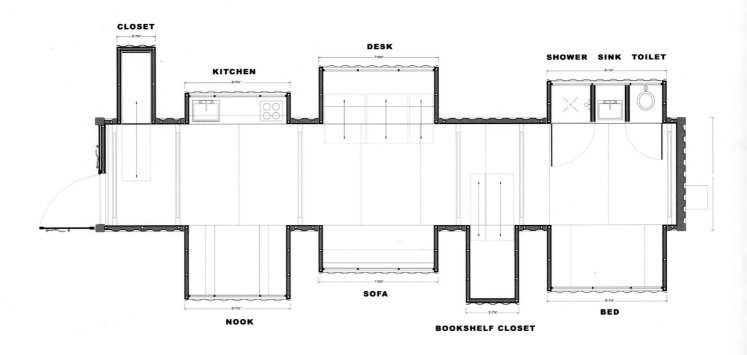

CLOSET

KITCHEN

DESK

SHOWER   SINK   TOILET

SOFA

NOOK

BOOKSHELF CLOSET

BED

Fig. 6.22 MDU. LOT-EK.

Fig. 6.23 Lafayette Tower. LOT-EK.

Fig. 6.24 MDU (Mobile Dwelling Unit), 1999. LOT-EK.

The A-Z Body Processing Unit

Fig. 6.25 Prototype for Processing Unit, 1993. Andrea Zittel.

Fig. 6.26 A-Z Cellular Compartment Unit, 2001. Andrea Zittel.

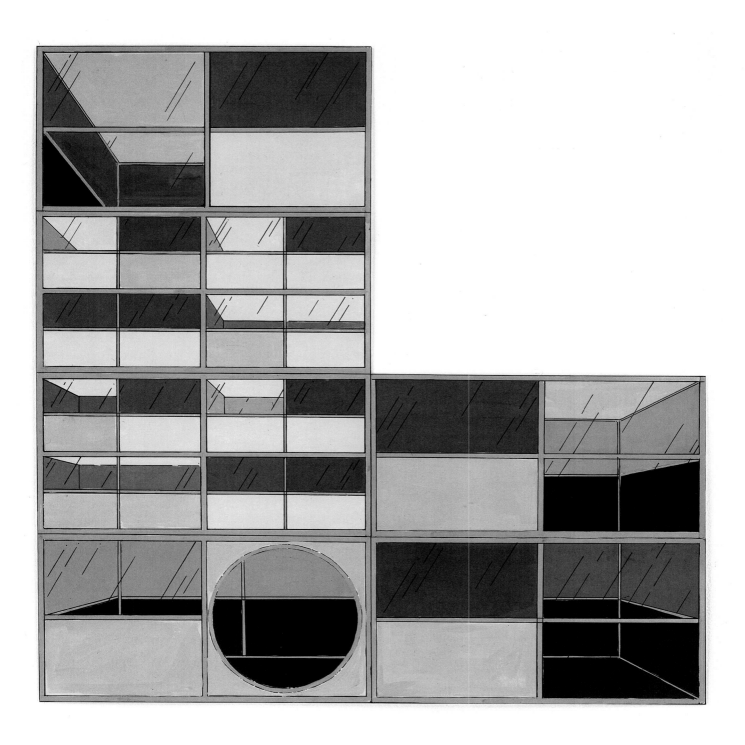

Fig. 6.27 Study for A - Z Cellular Compartment Units #6, 2002.
Andrea Zittel.

Fig. 6.28 High Rise, 1980. Vito Acconci.

Fig. 6.29 Park up a Building, Centro Galego de Arte Contemporánea, Santiago de Compostela, 1996. Acconci Studio: Vito Acconci, Luis Vera, Jenny Schrider and Charles Doherty.

Fig. 6.30 Times Square, NYC, 2002.

Fig. 6.31 KriegsZustand, from Truisms, Inflammatory Essays; laser projection, Leipzig, 1996. Jenny Holzer.

Fig. 6.32 Truisms, painted wall, Kassel, 1982. Jenny Holzer.

Fig. 6.33 "Monument" for V. Tatlin I, 1964. Dan Flavin.

Fig. 6.34 Keith Sonnier at Caltrans District 7 Building,
Los Angeles, 2004. Thom Mayne/Morphosis.

Fig. 6.35 Caltrans District 7 Building. Thom Mayne/Morphosis.

Fig. 6.36 Tower of the Winds, Yokohama, 1986
(dismantled 1995). Toyo Ito.

Fig. 6.37 Museum of Modern Art, Doug Aitken Projections,
New York City, 2007. Doug Aitken.

Fig. 6.38 Manhattan Air Rights, 2007. Doug Aitken.

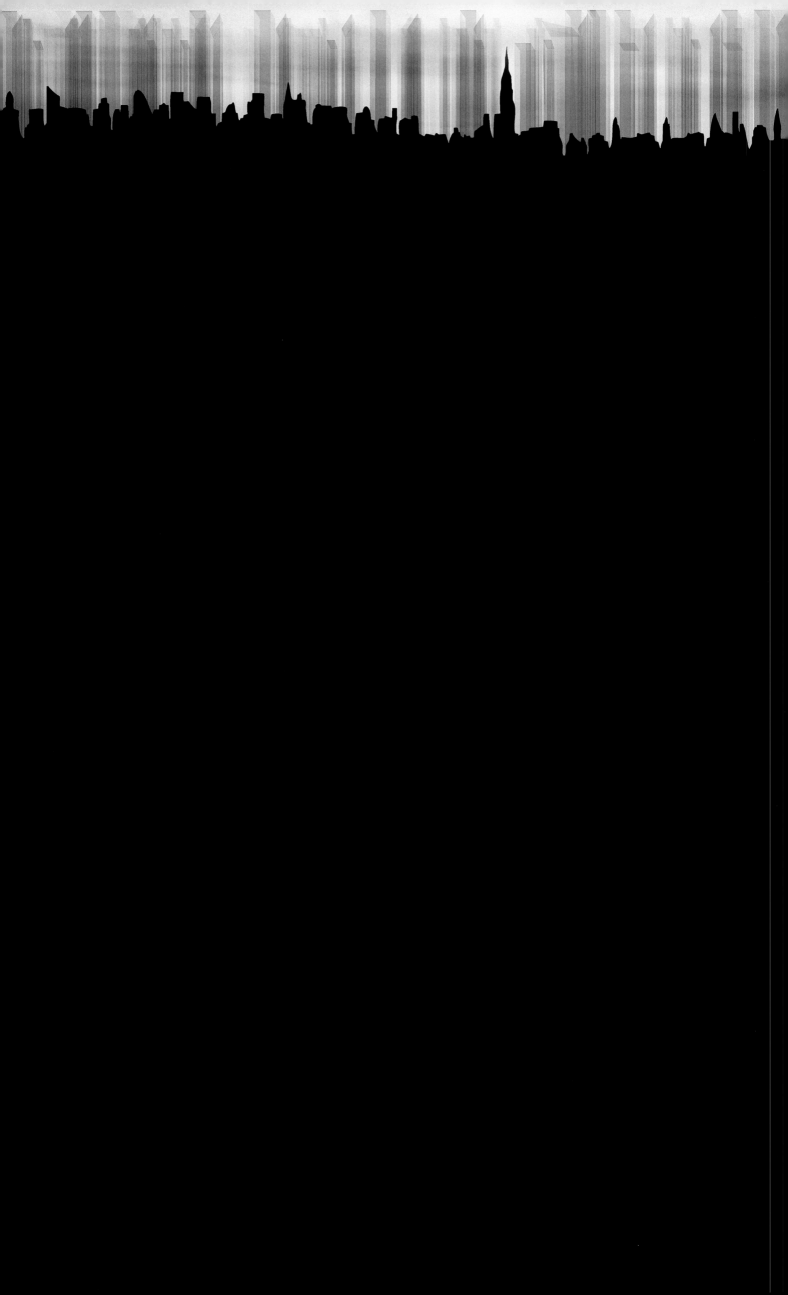

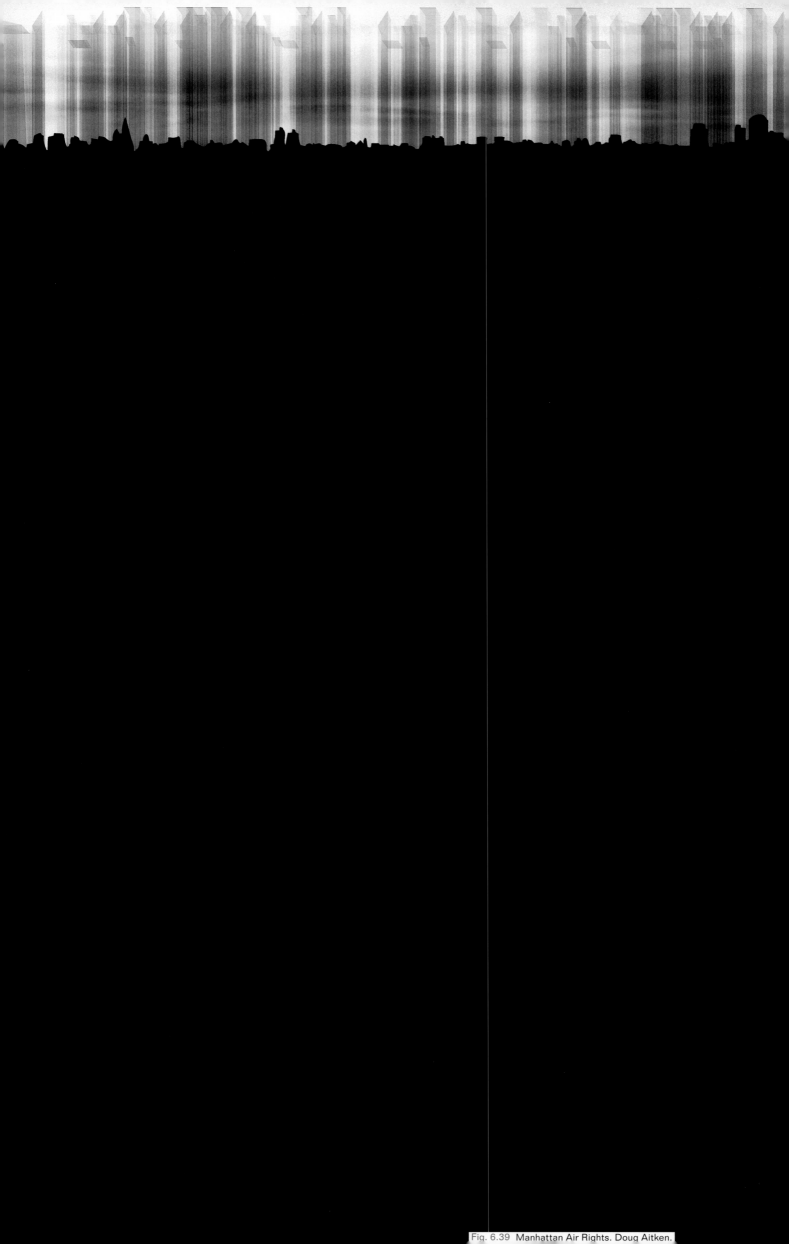

Fig. 6.39 Manhattan Air Rights. Doug Aitken.

Bibliography

Abalos, Inaki and Juan Herreros. *Tower and Office: From Modernist Theory to Contemporary Practice.* Cambridge, MA: The MIT Press, 2003.

Abramson, Daniel M. *Skyscraper Rivals: The AIG Building and the Architecture of Wall Street.* New York: Princeton Architectural Press, 2001.

Aitken, Doug. *Sleepwalkers.* New York: Museum of Modern Art, 2007.

Aldeasa, Ana Cela and Ana Martin. *Jean Nouvel.* Madrid: Museo Nacional, 2002.

Amelar, Sarah. *"Hearst Tower, New York City." Architectural Record: Green by Design.* August 2006: 74.

Antonelli, Paola. *Workspheres: Design and Contemporary Work Styles.* New York: The Musem of Modern Art, 2001.

Arnold, Wayne. "The Nanny State Places a Bet." *The New York Times.* May 23, 2006: C1.

Auge, Marc. *Non-Places, Introduction to an Anthropology of Supermodernity.* London: Verso, 1995.

Avins, Mimi. "L.A.'s high-style high-rise." *Los Angeles Times.* December 22, 2005: F1.

Bardeschi, Marco Dezzi. *Frank Lloyd Wright.* Firenze: G. C. Sansoni, 1970.

Baudrillard, Jean and Jean Nouvel. *The Singular Objects of Architecture.* Minneapolis: University of Minnesota Press, 2002.

Beadle, Lynn. *Tall Buildings and Urban Habitat.* London: Spon, 2001.

Béret, Chantal. *Jean Nouvel.* Barcelona: Actar, 2002.

Betsky, Aaron. *Violated Perfection.* New York: Rizzoli, 1990.

Binder, Georges. *101 of the World's Tallest Buildings.* Victoria: Images Publishing Group, 2006.

Binder, Georges. *Sky High Living: Contemporary High-Rise Apartment and Mixed-Use Buildings.* Australia: The Images Publishing Group Pty Ltd, 2002.

Binder, Georges. *Tall Buildings of Europe, Middle East & Africa.* Victoria: Images Publishing Group Pty, Ltd., 2007.

Boesiger, Willy (ed.). *Le Corbusier.* New York: Praeger Publishers, 1972.

Borges, Jorge, et.al. *Labyrinths, Selected Stories & Other Writings.* New York: New Directions, 2007.

Brownell, Blaine. "The Leaders of the Latest Material Revolution." *Architectural Record Innovation: Norman Foster and the Hearst Corporation complete an 80-year-old vision.* November 2005: 36.

Burdett, Richard and Sarah Ichioka. *Cities: People, Society, Architecture.* New York: Rizzoli, 2006.

Celant, Germano and Monica Ramirez-Montagut. *Zaha Hadid.* New York: The Solomon R. Guggenheim Foundation, 2006.

Condit, Carl W. *The Chicago School of Architecture: A History of Commercial and Public Building in the Chicago Area, 1875-1925.* Chicago, Illinois: The University of Chicago Press, 1964.

Cooke, Catherine. *The Russian Avant-garde: Art and Architecture (Architectural Design Profile).* New Jersey: Wiley-Academy, 1983.

Culot, Maurice and Grenier, Lise. *Henri Sauvage 1873-1932.* Belgium: Archives d'Architecture Moderne, 1978.

Davis, Mike. *Planet of Slums.* London: Verso, 2006.

Davis, Mike and Daniel Monk. *Evil Paradises.* New York: New Press, 2007.

Dawson, Layla. *China's New Dawn.* London: Prestel Publishing, 2005.

Delevoy, Robert L., Vidler, Anthony and Others. *Rational Architecture.* Belguim: Archives d'Architecture Moderne, 1978.

Doordan, Dennis. *Twentieth-Century Architecture.* London: Laurence King, 2001.

Duffy, Francis. *The New Office.* London: Conran Octopus Limited, 1997.

Dunlap, David. "Developer offers First Look at Freedom Tower's Neighbors." *The New York Times.* September 8, 2006: A23.

Dupre, Judith. *Skyscrapers.* New York: Black Dog & Leventhal Publishers, 2001.

Eklund, Douglas, et.al. *Thomas Struth, 1977-2002.* Dallas: Dallas Museum of Art, 2002.

Etlin, Richard. *Modernism in Italian Architecture, 1890-1940.* Cambridge: MIT Press, 1991.

Ferriss, Hugh. *Power in Buildings – An Artist's View of Contemporary Architecture.* New York: Columbia University Press, 1953.

Flagge, Ingeberg. *Main Tower.* Germany: Verlag Ernst Wasmuth, 2000.

Form Magazine. May/June 2007.

Fortmeyer, Russell. "Big Ideas for a Little Planet." *Architectural Record: Green by Design.* August 2006: 60.

Fortmeyer, Russell. "Holland Performing Arts, Nebraska." *Architectural Record: Green by Design.* August 2006: 124.

Frampton, Kenneth. *Steven Holl, Architect.* London: Phaidon, 2003.

French, Leanne. "Mixed Greens." *Architectural Record: Green by Design.* August 2006: 174.

Garreta, Ariadna Alvarez. Skyscrapers. Barcelona: Atrium Group, 2004.

Giovannini, Joseph. "Luxembourg Philharmonie, Luxembourg." *Architectural Record: Green by Design.* August 2006: 118.

Gissen, David. *Big&Green: Toward sustainable architecture in the 21st century.* New York: Princeton Architectural Press, 2002.

Goldberger, Paul. The Skyscraper. New York: Alfred A. Knopf, 1982.

Goldstein, Ann and Diedrich Diederichsen. *A Minimal Future?.* Los Angeles: Museum of Contemporary Art, 2004.

Gonchar, Joann. "Rooftops Slowly, but Steadily, Start to Sprout." *Architectural Record: Green by Design.* August 2006: 135.

Goulet, Patrice. *Jean Nouvel.* Paris: Editions du Regard, 1994.

Hadid, Zaha. *Zaha Hadid.* New York: Solomon R.Guggenheim Foundation, 2006.

Hart, Sara. "An Icon is Completed After 80 Years: Part I." *Architectural Record Innovation: Norman Foster and the Hearst Corporation complete an 80-year-old vision.* November 2005: 20.

Hart, Sara. "Building a State-of-the-art Home: Part II." *Architectural Record Innovation: Norman Foster and the Hearst Corporation complete an 80-year-old vision.* November 2005: 24.

Harvard Design Magazine. Spring/Summer 2007.

Hasegawa, Yuko. *Kazuyo Sejima + Ryue Nishizawa Sanaa.* Milan: Electa Architecture, 2006.

Haughey, Richard M.. *Higher-Density Development: Myth and Fact.* Washington D.C.: ULI-the Urban Land Institute, 2005.

Hawthorne, Christopher. "Not a single condo in sight: Hearst headquarters and 7 World Trade Center symbolize an older idea of skyscraper as a place of commerce." *Los Angeles Times.* May 23, 2006: E1.

Hodge, Brooke, et.al. *Skin + Bones.* London: Thames & Hudson, 2006.

Holl, Steven. *Parallax.* New York: Princeton Architectural Press, 2000.

Hope, James. *ibdi: intelligent build & design innovations.* London, England: SPG Media Limited, 2005/2006.

Howler, Eric. *Skyscraper.* New York, NY: Universe Publishing, 2003.

Ibelings, Hans. *Supermodernism.* Amsterdam: NAi Publishers, 2002.

Jencks, Charles. *Skyscrapers-Skycities.* New York: Rizzoli International Publications Inc., 1980.

Jencks, Charles. *The Iconic Building.* New York: Rizzoli International Publications, Inc., 2005.

Jobse, Jonneke. *De Stijl Continued. The Journal Structure (1958-1964). An Artist's Debate.* Rotterdam: 010 Publishers, 2005.

Joch, Alan and Deborah Snoonian. "Design Embraces the Machine Age." *Architectural Record Innovation: Norman Foster and the Hearst Corporation complete an 80-year-old vision.* November 2005: 30.

Jodidio, Philip. *Sir Norman Foster.* Italy: Taschen, 1997.

Johnson, Philip and Mark Wigley. *Deconstructivist Architecture.* Boston: Little, Brown, 1988.

Johnson, Scott. *The Big Idea, Criticality and Practice in Contemporary Architecture.* Glendale: Balcony Media, 2006.

Joselit, David, et.al. *Jenny Holtzer.* London: Phaidon, 1998.

Khan-Magomedov, S. *Alexandr Vesnin and Russian Constructivism.* New York: Rizzoli, 1986.

Kipnis, Jeffrey and Todd Gannon. *The Light Construction Reader.* New York: Monacelli, 2002.

Koolhaas, Rem. *Delirious New York.* New York: Monacelli Press, 1994.

Koolhaas, Rem. *Delirious New York: A Retroactive Manifesto for Manhattan.* New York: Oxford University Press, 1978.

Kostof, Spiro. *A History of Architecture.* New York: Oxford University Press, 1985.

Kurokawa, Kisho. *Metabolism and Symbiosis.* Berlin: Jovis Verlag GmbH, 2005.

Landau, Sarah and Carl Condit. *Rise of the New York Skyscraper, 1865-1913.* New Haven: Yale University Press, 1996.

Leich, Jean and Hugh Ferriss. *Architectural Visions.* New York: Whitney Library of Design, 1980.

Lepik, Andres. *Skyscrapers.* Munich: Prestel Verlag, 2004.

Lucan, Jacques. *Rem Koolhaas OMA.* New York: Princeton Architectural Press, 1996.

Lynn, Greg, et.al. *Tracing Eisenman.* New York: Rizzoli, 2006.

Lyotard, Jean. *The Postmodern Condition.* Minneapolis: University of Minnesota Press, 1984.

Machado, Rodolfo and Rodolphe el-Khoury. *Monolithic Architecture.* London: Prestel Publishing, 1996.

Matsuba, Kazukiyo. *Visual Architecture* "Artelligent City: Special Issue: The Mori Building Challenge March 2004 vol.40 305.

Morsiani, Paola. *Andrea Zittel.* London: Prestel Publishing, 2005.

Moudry, Roberta. *The American Skyscraper.* Cambridge: Cambridge University Press, 2005.

Muschamp, Herbert. "Urban Renewal: What is the modern skyline if not a reflection of male vanity?" Hedi Slimane builds a better skin-care system." *The New York Times Magazine.* September 3, 2006: 48.

Neumann, Dietrich and Donald Albrecht. *Film Architecture.* Munich: Prestel, 1996.

Noever, Peter (Editor), Donald Judd, Rudi Fuchs. *Donald Judd: Architecture: Architektur.* Ostfildern-Ruit: Hatje Cantrz, 2004.

Ouroussoff, Nicolai. "At Ground Zero, Tower for Forgetting." *The New York Times.* September 11, 2006: B1.

Ouroussoff, Nicolai. "Injecting a Bold Shot of the New on the Upper East Side." *New York Times.* October 10, 2006: B1.

Overy, Paul. *De Stijl.* New York: E.P. Dutton and Co. Inc, 1969.

Pehnt, Wolfgang. *Expressionist Architecture.* London: Thames & Hudson, 1979.

Pelegrin-Genel, Elisabeth. *The Office.* Paris: Flammarion,1996.

Piano, Renzo. *On Tour with Renzo Piano.* Oxford Oxfordshire: Phaidon, 2004.

Pogrebin, Robin. "High-Rises That Have Low Impact on Nature." *The New York Times.* February 2, 2006: B1.

Pogrebin, Robin. "How Green is My Tower?" *The New York Times.* April 16, 2006: B1.

Powell, Kenneth. *30 St Mary Axe: A Tower for London.* London: Merrell Publishers Limited, 2006.

Powell, R, and K. Yeang. *Rethinking the Skyscraper.* London: Thames & Hudson, 1999.

Pryor, Philip E. "Green the Landscape." *Multifamily Trends.* January/February 2006: 44.

Riley, Terence. *Light Construction.* New York: Museum of Modern Art, 2003.

Riley, Terence, et.al. *Mies in Berlin.* New York: Museum of Modern Art, 2001.

Riley, Terence. *On-Site.* New York: Museum of Modern Art, 2006.

Riley, Terence. *Tall Buildings.* New York: Museum of Modern Art, 2005.

Robinson, Cervin and Rosemarie Haag Bletter. *Skyscaper Style: Art Deco New York.* New York, Oxford University Press, 1975.

Rosen, Laura. *Top of the City: New York's Hidden Rooftop World.* New York, Thames and Hudson, 1982.

Russell, James S. "Guthrie Theater, Minneapolis." *Architectural Record: Green by Design.* August 2006: 108.

Russell, James S. "The effervescing surface of the AGBAR TOWER is startling symbol Ateliers Jean Nouvel has created for Barcelona's newest commercial district." *Architectural Record.* January 2006: 89.

Sadler, Simon. *Archigram.* Cambridge: MIT Press, 2005.

Savi, Vittorio. *Less is More.* Barcelona: Actar, 1997.

Schmal, C, Peter, et.al. *Kisho Kurokawa.* Berlin: Jovis, 2005.

Scoates, Christopher. *Lot/Ek: Mobile Dwelling Unit..* New York: Distributed Art Publishers, Inc, 2003.

Scuri, Piera. *Late Twentieth Century Skyscrapers.* New York: Van Norstrand Reinhold, 1990.

Siegal, Jennifer. *Mobile – the Art of Portable Architecture.* New York: Princeton Architectural Press, 2002.

Slessor, Catherine. "National Assembly for Wales, Wales." *Architectural Record: Green by Design.* August 2006: 100.

Smith, Bryan and Alex Coull. *Tall Building Structures.* New York: Wiley, 1991.

Solaguren-Beascoa de Corral, Felix. *Arne Jacobsen.* Barcelona: Editorial Gustavo Gili, 1992.

Sonnier, Keith. *Public Commissions in Architecture.* Ostfildern: Hatje Cantz, 2000.

Sontag, Deborah. "The Hole in the City's Heart." *The New York Times.* September 11, 2006: Broken Ground.

Sorkin, Michael (ed.). *Analyzing Ambasz.* New York: Monacelli Press, 2004.

Stephens, Suzanne. "Federal Environmental Agency, Germany." *Architectural Record: Green by Design.* August 2006: 82.

Stephens, Suzanne. *Imagining Ground Zero: Official and Unofficial Proposals for the World Trade Center Site.* New York, NY: Rizzoli International Publications, Inc., 2004.

Stern, Jewel and John Stuart. *Ely Jacques Kahn, Architect.* New York: W.W. Norton, 2006.

Sullivan, C.C. "Robo Buildings: Pursuing the Interactive Envelope." *Architectural Record.* April 2006: 149.

Tafuri, Manfredo. *Architecture and Utopia.* Cambridge: MIT Press, 1976.

Tigerman, Stanley. *Chicago Tribune Tower Competition.* New York: Rizzoli, 1989.

Tolla, Ada, et.al. *Lot/Ek.* New York: Princeton Architectural Press, 2002.

Townsend, Chris and Bill Viola. *The Art of Bill Viola.* London: Thames & Hudson, 2004.

Tribe, Mark, et.al. *New Media Art.* Köln: Taschen, 2006.

Troy, Nancy. *The De Stijl Environment.* Cambridge: MIT Press, 1983.

Viladas, Pilar. "Window Box: John Pawson goes out on a limb." *The New York Times Magazine.* August 20, 2006: 46.

Visual Architecture. March 2004.

Ward, Frazer, et.al. *Vito Acconci.* Oxford: Phaidon, 2002.

Weaving, Andrew and Gibbs Smith. *High-Rise Living.* Layton: Gibbs Smith Publishers, 2004.

Weibel, Peter, et.al. *Disappearing Architecture, from Real to Virtual to Quantum.* Boston: Birkhauser, 2005.

Wells, Matthew. *Skyscrapers: Structure and Design.* New Haven, CT: Laurence King Publishing, 2005.

Willis, Carol. *Form Follows Finance: Skyscrapers and Skylines in New York and Chicago.* New York: Princeton Architectural Press, 1995.

Willis, Carol. "Green Towers for New York: From Visionary to Vernacular." *The Skyscraper Museum.* March 15, 2006. The Skyscraper Museum. August 8, 2006. http://www.skyscraper.org/EXHIBITIONS/GREEN_TOWERS/gt_main.htm

Wilson, Robert. *Monuments.* Hannover: Kestner-Gesellschaft, 1991.

Wilson, Robert, et.al. *Robert Wilson.* Barcelona: Poligrafa, 2002.

Wines, James. *Green Architecture.* Köln: Taschen, 2000.

Wines, James N. *Identity in Density.* Victoria: Images Publishing, 2006.

Wolff, Rita, et.al. *Rita Wolff, Watercolours, 1974-1985.* New York: St. Martin's Press, 1986.

Wood, Paul. *Conceptual Art.* New York: Delano Greenidge, 2002.

Xue, Charlie Q.L. *Building a Revolution – Chinese Architecture Since 1980.* Seattle: University of Washington Press, 2006.

Yeang, Ken. *Ecodesign: A Manual for Ecological Design.* Great Britain: Wiley-Academy, 2006.

Yeang, Ken. *Reinventing The Skyscraper: A Vertical Theory of Urban Design.* Great Britain: Wiley-Academy, 2002.

Yoshida, Nobuyuki. *A + U Special Edition Herzog & de Meuron.* Japan: a + u Publishing Co. Ltd., 2006.

Yoshida, Nobuyuki. (ed.). *Peter Zumthor* Architecture and Urbanism February 1998 Extra Edition. Tokyo: a + u Publishing Co., Ltd., 1998.

Zaera-Polo Alejandro. "High-Rise Phylum 2007." *Harvard Design Magazine.* Spring/ Summer 2007.

Zukowsky, John and Martha Thorne. *Masterpieces of Chicago Architecture.* New York: Rizzoli, 2004.

Zukowsky, John. *Chicago Architecture 1872-1922: Birth of a Metropolis.* Munich, Germany: Presetel-Verlag, 1987.

Zukowsky, John and Martha Thorne. *Skyscrapers, the New Millenium.* Munich: Prestel, 2000.

Photography Credits

Every reasonable attempt has been made to identify owners of copyright. Errors or omissions will be corrected in subsequent editions.

Prologue 1 Erich Lessing/Art Resource, NY Prologue 2 Digital Image © The Museum of Modern Art/Licensed by SCALA/Art Resource, NY Fig. 1.1 Commercial Photographic Co. Fig. 1.2 Carol Willis, Form Follows Finance. Fig. 1.3 Berenice Abbott/ Commerce Graphics Ltd., Inc., New York; The New York Public Library/Art Resource, NY Fig. 1.4 The Bank of New York Mellon Archives. Fig. 1.5 Historic American Buildings Survey Lester Jones, Photographer, July 31, 1940. Fig. 1.6 The New York Public Library/Art Resource, NY. Fig. 1.7 The Skyscraper Museum from Carol Willis, Form Follows Finance. Fig. 1.8 "Metropolis", Dover Publications, Inc., 1929; Collection of Scott Johnson, FAIA. Fig. 1. 9 © Peter Aaron/Esto. Fig. 1.10 + Fig. 1.11 + Fig. 1.12 © 2008 Artists Rights Society (ARS), New York/ADAGP, Paris/ FLC. Fig. 1.13 + Fig. 1.14 + Fig. 1.15 + Fig. 1.16 + Fig. 1.17 Digital Image © The Museum of Modern Art/ Licensed by SCALA/Art Resource, NY; © 2008 Artists Rights Society (ARS), New York/VG Bild-Kunst, Bonn. Fig. 1.18 © Al Boretto/Emporis.com. Fig. 1.19 UN/DPI Photo. Fig. 1.20 + Fig. 1.21 + Fig. 1.22 Ezra Stoller © Esto. Fig. 1.23 From J. K. Freitag, "Architectural Engineering" (2d ed.; New York: John Wiley & Sons, 1901). Fig. 1.24 Courtesy of Skidmore, Owings & Merrill LLP. Fig. 1.25 From Myron Goldsmith, "Buildings and Concepts" (New York: Rizzoli, 1987), pp. 144, 145. Fig. 1.26 Courtesy of Skidmore, Owings & Merrill LLP; Ezra Stoller © Esto. Fig. 1.27 Courtesy of Skidmore, Owings & Merrill LLP. Fig. 1.28 © Edward Jacoby. Fig. 1.29 United Architects. Fig. 2.1 New York Historical Society. Fig. 2.2 From "L'Illustrazione Italiana" (August 31, 1913). Fig. 2.3 Deutsche Kinemathek. Fig. 2.4 Avery Architectural and Fine Arts Library, Columbia University. Fig. 2.5 From Henri Sauvage, "Henry Sauvage 1873-1932" (Archives d'Architecture Moderne, 1978). Fig. 2.6 Avery Architectural and Fine Arts Library, Columbia University. Fig. 2.8 Newspaper Collection, The New York Public Library, Astor, Lenox and Tilden Foundations. Fig. 2.10 The Waldorf Astoria. Fig. 2.12 Walter Kilham, Jr. Fig. 2.13 Walter Kilham, Jr. Fig. 2.14 Walter Kilham, Jr. Fig. 2.15 Rockefeller Center, Inc. Fig. 2.16 © Peter Mauss/Esto. Fig. 2.17 + Fig. 2.18 + Fig. 2.19 + Fig. 2.20 + Fig. 2.21 + Fig. 2.22 © 2008 Artists Rights Society (ARS), New York/ADAGP, Paris/FLC. Fig. 2.23 Ezra Stoller © Esto. Fig. 2.24 © Wayne Andrews/Esto. Fig. 2.25 © The Frank Lloyd Wright Foundation, AZ; Artists Rights Society (ARS), NY. Fig. 2.26 Foster + Partners. Fig. 2.27 The Ron Herron Archive.

Fig. 2.28 Courtesy of Sir Peter Cook. Fig. 2.29 Renzo Piano Workshop/Richard Rogers Partnership. Fig. 2.30 © 2008 The Isamu Noguchi Foundation and Garden Museum, New York/Artists Rights Society (ARS), New York. Fig. 2.31 + Fig. 2.32 Courtesy of Eisenman Architects. Fig. 2.33 + Fig. 2.34 + Fig. 2.35 Office for Metropolitan Architecture (OMA). Fig. 2.36 Hans Werlemann. Fig. 2.37 + Fig. 2.38 Courtesy of Studio Daniel Libeskind. Fig. 2.39 Courtesy of Skidmore, Owings & Merrill LLP. Fig. 2.40 Office for Metropolitan Architecture (OMA). Fig. 2.41 Courtesy of Richard Meier & Partners Architects, Eisenman Architects, Gwathmey Siegel & Associates, Steven Holl Architects. Fig. 3.1 Richard Einzig/arcaid.co.uk. Fig. 3.2 + Fig. 3.3 Ken Kirkwood. Fig. 3.4 Foster + Partners. Fig. 3.5 Ian Lambot. Fig. 3.6 Foster + Partners. Fig. 3.7 Foster + Partners; © Dennis Gilbert/ VIEW. Fig. 3.8 + Fig. 3.9 Ian Lambot. Fig. 3.10 Foster + Partners. Fig. 3.11 © Nigel Young/ Foster + Partners. Fig. 3.12 Foster + Partners. Fig. 3.13 © Hilson Moran. Fig. 3.14 + Fig. 3.15 + Fig. 3.16 Foster + Partners. Fig. 3.17 + Fig. 3.18 + Fig. 3.19 + Fig. 3.20 + Fig. 3.21 + Fig. 3.22 + Fig. 3.23 + Fig. 3.24 + Fig. 3.25 © T. R. Hamzah & Yeang Sdn. Bhd. (Malaysia). Fig. 4.1 + Fig. 4.2 + Fig. 4.3 © Scott Frances/Esto. Fig. 4.4 Copyright dbox Inc. Fig. 4.5 Billboard Design by Pandiscio Co., Photography by Todd Eberle. Fig. 4.6 © Jock Pottle/Esto. Fig. 4.7 + Fig. 4.8 studio amd. Fig. 4. 9 Rendering by Archpartners. Fig. 4.10 studio amd. Fig. 4.11 © Peter Mauss/Esto. Fig. 4.12 Santiago Calatrava S.A./© David Sundberg/ Esto; Fig. 4.13 © David Sundberg/Esto, composite rendering by Michael Hsiung. Fig. 4.14 Design: Oppenheim Architecture + Design, Rendering: dbox Inc. Fig. 4.15 Related Companies, Architecture by Frank Gehry. Fig. 4.16 Courtesy of CityCenter Land, LLC. Fig. 4.17 Ian Schrager Company. Fig. 4.18 © David Seide. Fig. 4.19 Nic Lehoux. Fig. 4.20 Copyright dbox Inc. Fig. 5.1 + Fig. 5.2 Mori Building Co., Ltd. Fig. 5.3 © 2008 Thomas Struth. Fig. 5.4 + Fig. 5.5 Courtesy of Skidmore, Owings & Merrill LLP; Shinkenchiku-sha. Fig. 5.6 © Lara Swimmer/ Esto. Fig. 5.7 Courtesy of Ellerbe Becket. Fig. 5.8 Photo by Michael Portman. Fig. 5. 9 © Norman McGrath/Esto. Fig. 5.10 Courtesy of Steven Holl Architects and Solange Fabiano. Fig. 5.11 Courtesy of Skidmore, Owings & Merrill LLP and China Jin Mao Group Co., Ltd. Fig. 5.12 Office for Metropolitan Architecture (OMA). Fig. 5.13 Courtesy of Morphosis. Fig. 5.14 Courtesy of Skidmore, Owings & Merrill LLP; © Wolfgang Hoyt/Esto. Fig. 5.15 Photo courtesy of Kingdom Holding Co. Fig. 5.16 Courtesy of Jumeirah. Fig. 5.17 © Ateliers Jean Nouvel/Artefactory. Fig. 5.18 Courtesy of Jumeirah. Fig. 5.19 EMAAR Properties. Fig. 5.20 Moscow City Government, courtesy of Sergei L. Loiko. Fig. 5.21 Foster + Partners. Fig. 5.22 Courtesy of RMJM. Fig. 5.23 Courtesy of Studio Daniel Libeskind. Fig. 5.24

Index

Abalos, Inaki, 25
Acconci, Vito, 218–219, 248
Adler & Sullivan, 33, 60, 75
Agbar Tower, 216, 219, 230
Air circulation issues, 19
Aitken, Doug, 219–220, 258–261
Alcoa Building, 26
Ambasz, Emilio, 217, 237–239
Apartment buildings.
    See also Condominiums;
        Designer skyscrapers
    Athletic House with Terraces, 59, 70, 71
    terraced building proposal, 59, 72
    Unité d'Habitation, 62, 83–85, 217
Apollo Real Estate Advisors, 63
Aqua Tower, 149, 171
Arata Isozaki, 208
Archetype, 25–26, 49–55
Archigram, 64, 92
Architettura in Superficia; Materiali,
    Figure e Tecnologie della Nuove
    Facciate Urbane, 215
Art Museum Bregenz, 215, 228
Artistic Imperialism, 59
Arts Magazine cover, 214, 226
Arup, 26
Asian skyscrapers
China, 178–179
Hong Kong, 176–177, 179, 190, 193
Japan and Tokyo, 176–178
Kuala Lumpur, 179–180
Taiwan, 180
Associated Architects, 61
Athletic House, 59, 70, 71
Athletic House with Terraces, 59, 70, 71
Atkins, 180, 200
Auditorium Building, 60, 75
Augé, Marc, 215
Automobile access regulations, 25
A-Z Body Processing Unit, 218, 245
A-Z Cellular Compartment Unit, 218,
    245–247

Bank of America Tower, 111
Bank of China, 179, 193
BATC Signature Tower, 116
Beach House, 149
Becket, Ellerbe, 178, 191, 199
Bell, Larry, 223
Bibliothéque Nationale de France, 216, 229
The Big Idea: Criticality and Practice
    in Contemporary Architecture, 11–12
Black Square, 213, 221
Blade Runner film, 60
BLUE Residential Tower, 147, 163
Brown, J. O., 61
Brueghel, Pieter, 4
Building envelopes, 19, 36
Building of Cities, 20
Building of the Tower of Babel, 4
Bunshaft, Gordon, 23, 46, 180, 198
Burj Al Arab, 180, 200
Burj Dubai, 180, 181, 203
Burnham, Daniel Hudson, 29

Calatrava, Santiago, 147, 148–149, 164–165
Caltrans District 7 Building, 219, 254–255
Candilis-Josic-Woods, 63
Cap de la Marine skyscraper, 62, 82
Carpenter, James, 114
Carson, Rachel, 109
Cartesian Skyscraper, 20, 21, 25, 39
CCTV tower, Beijing, 26, 64–65, 96–97, 179,
    196
Central Park West, 145, 154–155
Charles Street Condominiums, 144, 152
Chestnut-Dewitt Apartments, 26, 51
Chiba Town Center, 217
Chicago
    Chicago Spire, 148-149
    Chicago Tribune Building, 19, 37
    designer buildings, 148-149
    height limit, 19
    mixed-use skyscrapers, 59, 60
    skyscraper development, 18-19
Childs, David, 178
Chinese skyscrapers, 178-179
Chomsky, Noam, 12
Chrysler Building, 20
Citicorp Building, 26, 54
Cities Moving, 64, 92
City Design According to Its Artistic
    Principles, 20
City Hall at The Hague, 65
CityCenter, Las Vegas, 149-150, 168-169
Climatroffice, 112, 120
Cluster City, 63
Colafranceschi, Daniela, 215
Commercial City, 181
Commercial effects on skyscraper archetype,
    26-28
Commerzbank Headquarters, 113, 124-125
Complexity and Contradiction in Architecture,
    23
Condé Nast Building, 111
Condominiums.
    See also Apartment buildings;
        Designer skyscrapers
    Charles Street Condominiums, 144, 152
    luxury products, 145-147
    Perry Street Condominiums, 144-145, 151
        153
    Urban Glass House, 146, 156-157
Conran, Terence, 177, 183
A Contemporary City for Three Million, 20, 21,
    38, 213
Conway Building, 30
Cook, Peter, 64, 92
Corbett, Harvey Wiley, 61, 81
Cosmopolitan Resort & Casino, 149
Creek Vean House, 112, 117
Cross-braced steel variations, 26, 50
Cube: Life Unstructured, 149, 166
Cubism, 213
Culture transforming into retail, 145-146

de Meuron, Pierre, 148, 170
de Saussure, Ferdinand, 12

The Death and Life of Great American Cities,
   23
Deconstructivism, 215
Delirious New York, 60, 66
Design with Nature, 115
*Designing with Nature: The Ecological Basis
   for Architectural Design,* 115
Dialectics of profit and imagination, 18-23
Die, 222
Doha High-Rise Office Building, 180, 201
Downtown Athletic Club, 61, 77
Dubai skyscrapers, 180-181, 200-203
Dundy, Elmer, 73
Durst Organization, 111
Dutch Pavilion, 99

East End Avenue apartments, 145
Eckstut, Stan, 150
Eco-Tech City, 116
Eiffel Tower, 60
80 South Street, 147, 164-165
Eisenman, Peter, 64, 65-66, 94-95, 104-105
el-Khoury, Rodolphe, 215
Empire State Building, 20
Energy. *See* Environmental issues
Energy Void, 64, 93
Environmental issues
   energy management regulations, 25
   energy usage, 108-109
   exterior skin of buildings, 110, 111
   Foster buildings, 112-114, 117-131
   glass building energy usage, 110
   LEED, 109, 111-112, 114
   lighting, 109-110
   Yeang buildings, 114-116
   Zero-Energy Building, 111
Equitable Life Assurance Society Building,
   19, 34
European skyscrapers, 20
Expressive form, 213
Exterior skin of buildings, 110, 111
"Eye that sees", 62, 87

Ferris, Hugh, 19, 36
Fiera Milano Redevelopment, 208
Films containing skyscrapers, 59-60
Finsterlin, Herman, 22, 110
The Five Points, 20-21
Flavin, Dan, 219, 253
Floor plans in Manhattan, 19, 30
Form Follows Finance, 26-27
40 Bond, 148, 170
40 Mercer Residences, 146-147, 158-159
Foster, Norman
   CityCenter, Las Vegas, 149-150, 168-169
   environmental skyscrapers, 112-114, 117-131
   Hearst Tower, 111, 114, 130-131
   Hong Kong and Shanghai Bank, 26, 112-113,
      121
   London tower, 26
   Millennium Tower, 63, 91
   Moscow City Tower, 182, 205
   Swiss Re building, 14, 26, 113, 126-129
Foster, Wendy, 112, 117-131

The Fountainhead film, 60
425 Fifth Avenue, 145
Fragrant Hill Hotel, 178
Freed, Pei Cobb, 179, 193
Freight access regulations, 25
Friedrichstrasse Skyscraper, 22, 40, 41
Fukuoka Prefectural International Hall, 217,
   238
Fuller, Buckminster, 110, 112, 120, 214, 226
Fuller Building, 29
*The Future Circulation and the Skyscrapers
   of New York,* 59, 68

Gazprom City, 182, 206-207
Gehry, Frank, 148, 167
Gherkin, 113-114. *See also* Saint Mary Axe
   (Swiss Re) building
Gibson, William, 217
Glass buildings, energy usage, 110
Glass Skyscraper, 22, 42, 43
Godley & Fouilhoux, 81
Goldsmith, Myron, 26, 50
Goldstein, Ann, 214
Graham, Bruce, 26, 52
Graham, Dan, 214
Gramercy Park Hotel, 147, 148
Grand Central Station, 59
Grattacielo, 11
Graves, Michael, 145
Great Wall Hotel, 178, 191
Groningen Forum, 209
Ground Zero, 65-66, 100-105
Gwathmey, Charles, 65-66, 104-105

Hard Rock Hotel, 149
Haring, Hugo, 22
Harrison, Wallace K., 23, 45, 61
Harrison & McMurray, 81
Hearst Tower, 111, 114, 130-131
Height and bulk regulations, 24
Herreros, Juan, 25
Herron, Ron, 64, 92
Herzog, Jacques, 148, 170
High Rise, 218, 248
Highrise of Homes, 216, 216-217, 233
Hilberseimer, Ludwig, 21-22, 110, 213
Hilton Hotels, 180
Hitechniaga Headquarters, 116, 138
Hofmeister, Henry, 61, 81
Holabird and Roche, 29, 49
Holl, Steven
   Linked Hybrid model, 179, 194
   Town Center Tower, 216, 231
   World Trade Center proposal, 65-66,
      104-105
Holzer, Jenny, 219, 251-252
Hong Kong and Shanghai Bank, 26, 112-113,
   121
Hong Kong skyscrapers, 176-177, 179, 190,
   193
Hood, Raymond, 19-20, 61, 78, 81
Hopkins, Michael, 178
Hospitality buildings, 147-148
House up a Building, 218-219
Howell, John Mead, 19

Ibelings, Hans, 215, 216
IBM Plaza, 115-116, 136
Icefall, 114
Iconic Building, 14
Illinois Institute of Technology, 214, 224
Impala, 145
Informational tower, 216-220
ITN Headquarters, 113, 122-123
Ito, Toyo, 219, 256-257

Jacobs, Jane, 23
Jacobsen, Arne, 214, 227
Jahn, Helmut, 149, 168-169
Japanese skyscrapers, 176-178
Jencks, Charles, 14, 214, 215
Jenney, William Le Baron, 29
The Jerde Partnership, 177, 183
Jin Lin Hotel, 178
Jin Mao Tower, 179, 195
John Hancock Center, 26, 53, 63
Johnny Mnemonic, 217
Johnson, Philip, 7, 47, 146, 156-157
Johnson Wax Research Tower, 63, 88
Johor Bahru, 116
Jumeirah Emirates Towers, 180-181, 202

Kengo Kuma, 179
Kettelhut, Erich, 69
Khan, Fazlur, 26, 52
Kilham, Walter, Jr., 79
King, Moses, 59, 67
Kingdom Centre, 199
Koolhaas, Rem
    CCTV tower, Beijing, 26, 64-65, 96-97, 179, 196
    Delirious New York, 60, 66
    new space inventory, 216
    World Trade Center proposal, 65-66, 103
KriegsZustand, 219, 251
Kuala Lumpur skyscrapers, 179-180

Lafayette Tower, 217, 243
Lang, Fritz, 59, 69
The Language of Post-Modern Architecture, 215
Las Vegas
    CityCenter, 149-150, 168-169
    designer buildings, 149-150
Le Corbusier
    Cap de la Marine skyscraper, 62, 82
    Cartesian Skyscraper, 20, 21, 25, 39
    A Contemporary City for Three Million, 20, 21, 38, 213
    "eye that sees", 62, 87
    The Five Points, 20-21
    glass towers, 110
    Plan Voisin, Paris, 20-21, 38
    Unité d'Habitation, 62-63, 83-85, 217
    United Nations building, 22-23, 45
    Viaduct Block, 217, 232
Le Messurier, William, 26, 54
Leadership in Energy and Environmental Design (LEED), 109, 111-112, 114
Less is More, Minimalism in Architecture and the Other Arts, 215

Lever House, 23, 46
LeWitt, Sol, 225
Libeskind, Daniel, 23, 65, 100, 101
Life building, 19
Light Construction, 215
Lighting
    artificial light, 219
    building planning, 19
    energy usage, 109-110
    natural lighting, 110-111
    windows, 109, 110
Lignano, Giuseppe, 217
Linked Hybrid model, 179, 194
London Bridge Tower, 63
London tower, 26
Look Building, 23, 44
Los Angeles residential towers, 148
LOT-EK, 217-218, 240-244
Luckman, Charles, 23
Luna Park, 60, 73
Luxury real estate, 144-147

Machado, Rodolfo, 215
Madison Avenue, 144-147
Maki, Fumihiko, 177, 183
Malevich, Kazimir, 213, 221
Mandarin Oriental Hotel, 148, 167
Manhattan
    floor plans, 19, 30
    floor plates, 19, 32
    Ground Zero, 65-66, 100-105
    Manhattan Air Rights Project, 220, 259-261
    Manhattan Building, 29
    skyline, 19, 31
Manifesto of Futurist Architecture, 59
Marinetti, Filippo Tommaso, 59
Marino, Peter, 145
Mat buildings, 63
Max Reinhardt Haus, 64, 94-95
Mayne, Thom, 197, 219, 254-255
MBf Tower, 116, 139
McHarg, Ian, 115
McShine, Kynaston, 214-215
Mega-structures, 63
Meier, Richard
    Beach House, 149
    designer skyscrapers, 144-145
    Perry Street Condominiums, 144-145, 151-153
    World Trade Center proposal, 65-66, 104-105
Menara Boustead, 116
Menara Mesiniaga, 116, 137
Menara UMNO, 116
Menzie, William Cameron, 59
Metaphors, 13-14
Metropolis, 69
Metropolis film, 59
Metropolitan building, 19
Metropolitan Opera House, 61
Metropolitan Square, 61, 78-80
Middle Eastern skyscrapers, 180-181
Millennium Tower, 63, 91
Miller Hull Partnership, 149, 172

Miller-Jones Studio, 217
Minimalism, 213-216
Mixed-use skyscrapers
    apartments, 59, 62-63
    background, 58-59, 60
    construction costs, 58-59
    development of, 60-64
    Ground Zero, 65-66, 100-105
    Jumeirah Emirates Towers, 180-181, 202
    mega-structures, 63
    modern designs, 63-64
    Moskva-City, 181-182, 204
    post-war designs, 64-65
    Rockefeller Center, 20, 61-62, 78, 81
    shown in films, 59-60
    visions for uses, 59
    Waldorf Astoria Hotel, 60-61, 76
Mixer, 218
Mobile Dwelling Unit, 217, 218, 240-242, 244
Modernism, 145, 213-216
Moment frame, 25-26
Monolithic Architecture, 215
Montaner, Josep M., 215
Monument for V, 219, 253
Monument Tower Offices, 217, 239
Morasso, Mario, 59
Mori Building Co., Ltd., 177, 183-185
Morphosis, 7, 197, 219, 254-255
Morris, Benjamin Wistar, 78
Morton, Peter, 149
Moscow City Tower, 182, 205
Moses, Robert, 23
Moskva-City, 181-182, 204
Murphy/Jahn, 149
Museum of Modern Art, 219-220, 258

National Commerce Bank, 180, 198
The New Mechanical Aspect of the World, 59
New York City
    apartments, 145
    commercial office space, 18-19
    energy-efficient buildings, 111
    Madison Avenue, 144-147
    Manhattan. See Manhattan
    mixed-use skyscrapers, 59, 60
    public vision and capitalist drive of buildings,
        20
    real estate prices, 146
    skyscraper development, 19
    Study of Economic Height for Office
        Buildings, 19, 35
    zoning ordinance, 19, 23, 220
New York Times Headquarters, 111
Nichii Obihiro Department Store, 217, 237
Nobel, Philip, 217
Noguchi, Isamu, 64, 93
Non-Places, Introduction to an Anthropology
    of Supermodernity, 215
Nordenson, Guy, 13
Norton, Enrique, 150, 173
Nouvel, Jean
    Agbar Tower, 216, 219, 230
    Doha High-Rise Office Building, 180, 201
    40 Mercer Residences, 146-147, 158-161

100 11th Avenue residential tower, 146-147,
    160-161

Office for Metropolitan Architecture (OMA)
    CCTV tower, Beijing, 26, 64-65, 96-97, 179,
        196
    Sea Trade Center in Zeebrugge, 65, 98
    triangulated buildings, 26
    World Trade Center proposal, 66, 103
Old Colony Building, 26, 29, 49
Omrania & Associates, 199
One York Enrique Norten, 150, 173
100 11th Avenue residential tower, 146-147,
    160-161
156 West Superior, 149, 172
One-Mile-High Skyscraper, 63, 90
Open space regulations, 24
Oppenheim, Chad, 149, 166

Palace of Vertical Gardens, 217
Palmer & Turner, 178
Pandiscio, Richard, 146
Paris, A Contemporary City for Three Million,
    20, 21, 38
Park up a Building, 218-219, 249
Pawson, John, 147, 150
Peachtree Center, 64
Pearl River Tower, 111
Pedersen, Kohn, Fox Associates, 149,
    168-169, 177, 183-185
Pei, I. M., 178
Pei Cobb Freed & Partners Bank of China, 26
Pelli, Cesar, 26, 111, 149, 168-169
Pentagonal site, 22, 42, 43
Peoples Gas Company Building, 30
Permeability regulations, 24-25
Perrault, Dominique, 216, 229
Perreault, Jean, 214
Perret, Auguste, 20
Perry Street Condominiums, 144-145, 151-153
Petronas Towers, 26, 179-180
Pettit, Harry M., 67
Phare Tower of Morphosis, 7, 197
Photomontage, 216, 234
Piano, Renzo, 63, 92, 111
Plan Voisin, Paris, 20-21, 38
Playtime film, 60
Plaza Atrium, 115, 134-135
Plug-In City, 64, 92
Poelzig, Hans, 22
Pompidou Centre, 92
Portman, John, 64, 179, 192
Post-criticality, 12
Postmodernism, 215
Post-structuralism, 11-12
Post-war designs, 64-65
Price Tower, 63, 89
Prouve, Jean, 110
Public improvement regulations, 25

Radio Corporation of America (RCA) Building,
    61
Railway Exchange Building, 30
Rand-MacNally Building, 30

Regalia, 149
Regulations
    context and consensus, 24-25
    New York City zoning ordinances, 19, 23, 220
The Reichstag, 113
Reinhard, Andrew, 61, 81
Related Companies, The, 63
Reliance Building, 110
Residence Mumbai, 217, 236
Residential towers. See Apartment buildings;
    Condominiums; Designer skyscrapers
Retail of luxury products, 145-147
Reticulated towers, 25
Riley, Terence, 215-216
RMJM, 182, 206-207
Robertson, Hugh, 61
Rockefeller, John D., 61
Rockefeller Center, 20, 61-62, 78, 81
Rockwell Group, 162
Rogers, 92
Rogers, Richard, 112-114, 117-131
Roof-Roof House, 115, 132-133
Roppongi Hills, 177, 183-185
Russian skyscrapers, 181-182

Saint Mary Axe (Swiss Re) building, 14, 26,
    113-114, 126-129
Sant'Elia, Antonio, 59
Sarazin, Charles, 59, 70, 71
SAS Royal Hotel, 227
Sauvage, Henri, 59, 70, 71
Savi, Vittorio, 219
Scharoun, Hans, 26
Scheerbart, Paul, 26, 114
Schiedhelm, Manfred, 67
Schrager, Ian, 151-152, 154
Schultze & Weaver, 64, 80
Scott, Ridley, 64
Sea Trade Center in Zeebrugge, 69, 102
Seagram Building, 27, 51, 218
Sears Tower, 30, 56
Selldorf, 161
Semper, Gottfried, 114
Sendai Mediatheque, 223
Serial Project, 229
Series One Towers, 119
Series Two Towers, 120
Sert, Jose Luis, 67
75 Wall Street, 166
Shade and shadow regulations, 28
Shanghai Armoury Tower, 120
Shanghai Bank, 30
Shanghai Centre, 183, 196
Shinju-ku, Tokyo, 190-191
Shin-Marunouchi Building, 182
Shreve, Lamb & Harmon, 24
Significant form, 217
Silent Spring, 113
Singer building, 23, 114
Sirota, Gennady, 208
SITE, 220-221, 237-240, 240
Sitte, Camillo, 24
Sixth Avenue, NYC, skyscrapers, 27, 52

Skidmore, Owings & Merrill (SOM)
    Alcoa Building, 30
    Burj Dubai, 184, 185, 207
    Chestnut-Dewitt Apartments, 30, 55
    Ground Zero plan, 69, 106
    Jin Mao Tower, 183, 199
    John Hancock Center, 30, 57, 67
    Lever House, 27, 50
    National Commerce Bank, 184, 202
    Pearl River Tower, 115
    Tokyo Midtown, 182, 182-193
Smith, Adrian, 185, 207
Smith, Tony, 226
Smithson, Alison and Peter, 67
Solaire, 115
Sonnier, Keith, 223
Sorkin, Michael, 221
Space issues, 23
Standard model, 17
Starrett, Theodore, 64, 65, 76, 81
Stern, Robert A. M., 27, 115, 149
Structuralism, 15
Struth, Thomas, 180, 190-191
Stubbins, Hugh, 30, 58
Studio Daniel Libeskind, 212
Studio Gang Architects, 153, 175
Study of Economic Height for Office Buildings,
    23, 39
Style, in the Technical and Tectonic Arts: or,
    Practical Aesthetics, 114
Sullivan, Louis, 23, 37
SuperModernism: Architecture in the Age of
    Globalization, 220
Sustainability regulations, 29
Swanke Hayden Connell Architects, 186
Swiss Re building, 18, 30, 170, 130-133

Tafuri, Manfredo, 28
Taipei 101, 180
Taiwanese skyscrapers, 180
Tati, Jacques, 60
Tatlin, Vladimir, 4
Taut, Bruno, 22, 110
Team Ten, 63
Temporal, Marcel, 20
Things to Come film, 59
Third International, 1919, monument, 4
Thompson, Frederic, 60, 73
Times Square, 219, 250
Todd, John, 61
Tokyo skyscrapers
    current trends, 177
    Tokyo Midtown, 178, 188-189
    Tokyo-Nara Tower, 116
Tolla, Ada, 217
Tower City, 20
Tower of Babel, 4
Tower of the Winds, 219, 256-257
Town Center Tower, 216, 231
Trajectories, 58-64
Triangular commercial site, 22, 40, 41
Triangular design, 26, 112, 113, 182
Tribeca Green, 111
Truisms, 219, 252

Trump, 150
Tschumi, Bernard, 147, 163
Typological phylum, 27

Unité d'Habitation, 62-63, 83-85, 217
United Nations building, 22-23, 45
United States Green Building Council
   (USGBC), 109. See also Leadership in Energy
   and Environmental Design (LEED)
Universiti Telekom Multimedia Campus, 140
UNStudio, 209
Urban Glass House, 146, 156-157
Urbanisme, 20

van Alen, William, 20
van der Rohe, Ludwig Mies, 21
   archetype, 25
   art skyscrapers, 214
   glass towers, 110
   Illinois Institute of Technology, 214, 224
   pentagonal site, 22, 42, 43
   Seagram Building, 23, 47, 214
   triangular site, 22, 40, 41
Van Eyck, Aldo, 63
Van Vleck, 61, 77
Ventilation
   glass buildings, 110-111
   Hearst Tower, 114
   vertical ventilation flue, 113
Venturi, Robert, 23
Vers une Architecture, 20
Vertical truss, 26
Viaduct Block, 217, 232
Vidor, King, 60
Vinoly, Rafael, 149, 168-169

Wainwright Building, 33
Waldorf Astoria Hotel, 60-61, 76
Walking City, 64
Water Tower Place, 64
Waterfront Tower, 141
Wedding cake skyscrapers, 19, 66
Weinrich, John, 80
Wigley, Mark, 111
Willis, Carol, 26-27
Willis Faber and Dumas Office, 112-114,
   118-119
Windows
   energy efficiency, 110
   natural lighting, 109-110
   Saint Mary Axe building, 114
Wines, James, 216
Wolton, Georgie, 112-114, 117-131
Wong, Hazel, 180-181, 202
Woolworth Building, 7, 19, 110
World Exposition in Paris, 60
World Trade Center
   Ground Zero, 65-66, 100-105
   proposals, 65-66, 100-105
   Site Competition, 26, 55
   terrorist attacks, 7
Worldbridge Trade and Investment Center, 217
Wright, Frank Lloyd
   Johnson Wax Research Tower, 63, 88

One-Mile-High Skyscraper, 63, 90
Price Tower, 63, 89

Yeang, Ken, 7, 114-116, 132-141

Zaera-Polo, Alejandro, 27
Zaha Hadid, 208
Zero-Energy Building (ZEB), 111
Zhu Pei, 179
Zittel, Andrea, 218, 245-247
Zoning ordinances
   context and consensus, 24-25
   in New York City, 19, 23, 220
Zumthor, Peter, 228

Acknowledgements

I wish to thank a number of people who contributed in various ways to the creation of this book. Key among them are my colleagues at Johnson Fain, who through our work together and continuing conversations, challenge me to understand the design of tall buildings in new ways. My partner, Bill Fain, deserves appreciation for providing critical input into my obsession with building design and the urban environment in which these buildings reside. Mark Gershen always provides thoughtful edits to text and Cherie Miller, my assistant, coordinates many of the resources which support an effort such as this. Julie Bandini, Dana Smith, Joel Hernandez and Allen Wong have done much in the matter of gathering visual materials and securing the necessary copyrights.

Thanks go out to my publisher, Ann Gray at Balcony Media, for her many insights and support. My colleague, Dennis Doordan, architecture and design historian at the University of Notre Dame, offered invaluable suggestions to the early text. Richard Weinstein, architect, professor and former Dean of the School of Architecture and Urban Planning at the University of California, Los Angeles provided me my first teaching opportunity to survey tall buildings in Los Angeles, at the time, an anomalous city from which to make a grand survey of skyscrapers.

I would like to thank the University of Southern California School of Architecture, where I teach a range of classes, including design and critical theory. In design, I was privileged to teach the first recent high-rise studio 3 years ago. It was both a challenging and exhilarating semester with students attempting to become technically informed enough to be relevant yet expansive enough to explore the tall building's conceptual possibilities. The energy level and output of the studio was exemplary. I wish to thank the current dean of the School, Qingyun Ma for his progressive leadership of the institution and his efforts to unite a global perspective, big ideas and design processes. For the characteristically spirited and insightful preface, I thank Peter Cook.

Jean-Marc Durviaux and his associates at DISTINC have brought superior graphic art to this project and I've enjoyed the collaboration. They have provided both a highly ordered view of the book's content as well as an elegant approach to the wide range of ideas which are undertaken here.

Lastly, in the area of tall building design, I am indebted to a host of creative practitioners ranging from William Le Messurier, Chuck Basset, Marc Goldstein, Philip Johnson, John Burgee, and William Pereira. Each had a distinct vision of the possibilities inherent in the design of tall buildings. Their willingness to generously share the sources of their enthusiasm has taught me to discover my own.

The Author

Scott Johnson is an architect and founder of Johnson Fain, an international design practice based in Los Angeles. He is a professor of architecture at the University of Southern California and the author of the recent book, *THE BIG IDEA, Criticality and Practice in Contemporary Architecture* (2006 Balcony Press). Mr. Johnson grew up in California and was first exposed to tall buildings as a child in San Francisco. Following studies at Stanford University and graduation from the College of Environmental Design at the University of California at Berkeley, he accepted an apprenticeship position with a local firm in San Francisco adjacent to Willis Jefferson Polk's 1918 Hallidie Building on Sutter Street. Although only eight stories in height, the structure has been identified as the first known commercial building to adapt an all-glass and iron curtain wall technology from earlier industrial structures.

Mr. Johnson attended the Harvard School of Design during the years of the construction of I.M. Pei's John Hancock Center in Boston, a sixty-story building whose opening was long delayed due to the adverse effects of wind pressures and foundation settlement. Concurrently, he was a student of William LeMessurier, the preeminent structural engineer responsible for some of America's tallest and most iconic towers. While at Harvard, he also worked at The Architects' Collaborative, the architectural office founded by Walter Gropius and, at the time, occupied with the design and construction of several tall buildings in Boston.

Following graduation from Harvard, Mr. Johnson returned to California for two years, where he worked for Skidmore, Owings & Merrill under the supervision of Charles Bassett, the principal designer of the Crown Zellerbach Building and the Alcoa Building, two of San Francisco's first generation of modern skyscrapers, as well as Marc Goldstein, designer of the Bank of America Tower, at the time, the tallest building in the city.

Subsequently, Mr. Johnson returned to the East Coast, where he worked as a design associate for Philip Johnson, then Johnson Burgee Architects located in the Seagram Building, on a range of tall buildings, beginning with New York City's AT&T Building, Republic Bank Center and Transco Tower in Houston, International Place at Fort Hill Square in Boston, and 885 Third Avenue (the Lipstick Building) and proposals for the Times Square Redevelopment Project. While with Philip Johnson, Scott Johnson acted as assistant to Arthur Drexler, Director of Architecture & Design at the Museum of Modern Art, on the 1982 exhibition, "Three New Skyscrapers," featuring tall buildings by Philip Johnson, Norman Foster and Gordon Bunshaft.

Relocating to Los Angeles in the mid-1980s, Mr. Johnson assumed the role of director of design for William Pereira, the architect of San Francisco's Transamerica Pyramid. Mr. Johnson's first design commission with the California-based firm that has since become Johnson Fain was for a forty-story office tower to house the 20th

Century Fox Film Corporation named Fox Plaza and later widely featured in that studio's major motion picture, *Die Hard.* The completion of that project led to additional commissions for high-rise buildings, notably San Francisco's Rincon Center, a twin residential tower project that included the restoration of the historic Rincon Postal Annex and was chronicled in Douglas Franz's 1991 book, *From the Ground Up.* In Southern California, Mr. Johnson is known as the designer of tall buildings such as SunAmerica Center, MGM Tower and the Nestlé headquarters, and he is currently designing skyscrapers in Japan, China, Texas and San Diego, as well as a new generation of mixed-use residential towers throughout the Los Angeles region.

Published in the United States of America
in 2008 by Balcony Press.

For information address Balcony Media, Inc.
512 E. Wilson Avenue, Suite 213, Glendale
California 91206.

Design by DISTINC
Printing and production by
Navigator Cross-Media
Printed in South Korea

Library of Congress
Control Number: 2008934541
ISBN 978-1-890449-47-6